Omelette

Omelette

*Food, Love, Chaos
and Other Conversations*

Jessie Ware

HODDER*studio*

First published in Great Britain in 2021 by Hodder Studio
An Hachette UK company

2

Copyright © Jessie Ware 2021

A CIP catalogue record for this title is available from the British Library

Hardback ISBN 9781529355857
eBook ISBN 9781529355864

Typeset in Electra LT by Hewer Text UK Ltd, Edinburgh
Printed and bound in Great Britain by Clays Ltd, Elcograf S.p.A.

Hodder & Stoughton policy is to use papers that are natural, renewable
and recyclable products and made from wood grown in sustainable
forests. The logging and manufacturing processes are expected to
conform to the environmental regulations of the country of origin.

Hodder & Stoughton Ltd
Carmelite House
50 Victoria Embankment
London EC4Y 0DZ

www.hodder-studio.com

For my mum, Lennie, who makes everything so full of love, laughter and most importantly, food (even at times when it shouldn't be possible)

Introduction

As soon as I came out of my mother, I was so greedy that I made her nipples bleed.

My grandfather, Mor Mor, had to go to the hospital pharmacy and furtively whisper the words 'nipple guards' over the counter to get her something to ease the pain. It was mortifying for him. This story is regularly used by my mother as a segue before she proudly explains to a stranger that my party trick is remembering any dish we have ever had on any holiday. That's how much I like my food. From day one, nothing was going to stop us having the strongest bond – food has always been an inextricable part of my personality. Before I could talk, my toes would wiggle in the high chair anticipating the incoming plate; I would gladly finish my siblings' leftovers; I would want to know what was for dinner when we were only just sitting down for breakfast, and I would wait around in the kitchen watching my mother cook, like a dog waiting for scraps to fall.

This book is not my whole life, but rather a series of snapshots of some of my most formative experiences. Food is my strongest conduit to memory. I look back on how it has been threaded through my life and been a guest at some of my most important moments. Sometimes with music, often with family and friends, occasionally appearing while growing up during the nineties and noughties. But at the centre of each story is food, always food.

Food started as a necessity but has grown to become many things: a gift from my mother; a part of growing up; an act of love; an accompaniment through the strange world of work and celebrity; a way of understanding myself as a young woman, and now as a mother.

I don't need an excuse to order an entire menu, but writing a book about food memories has given me extra licence to do so. Apparently, I can say that I am writing a 'foodoir', a category I never knew existed and a word I'm not sure I'm completely comfortable with, but as long as it provides an incentive to eat . . .

To eat gives me more pleasure than anything, perhaps even more than music. But add music to the act of eating and that is alchemy of crescendoing delight. I live to eat; I do not eat to live.

Spaghetti Bolognese

M ad cow disease was good for one thing and one thing only: the short-lived birth of my mum's lamb bolognese. The COVID-19 pandemic has made mad cow disease sound like a Disney show, but in 1993 it was front-page news: 100,000 cows were infected with it and everyone was laying off beef. People were panicking, though not every poor sod had to have their parents' fear emblazoned on a knit. I remember a girl in my class with a sign pinned onto her jumper that said 'DO NOT FEED THIS CHILD BEEF' in bold marker pen. My mum started to make lamb bolognese so as not to disrupt our weekly menu too severely. It tasted thicker, richer and more exciting than her pressure-cookered beef version – I lapped it up. She cooked it on the stove in our 1970s plastic-walled chalet in Abersoch, Wales, in the Easter holidays, the minced meat hard to see through the sea of red oil lying on the top. I would stealthily dig into spoonful upon spoonful of lukewarm bolognese from the pan all afternoon, full by supper two hours later. Of course, I still ate a full meal. Such is the power of a bolognese, beef or lamb, whichever way you like it.

Everyone's is different, everyone's has a twist. A dash of milk; pork, veal or beef mince; white wine instead of red; balsamic vinegar; a beef Oxo cube; a splash of Lea & Perrins; cinnamon; mushrooms, carrots, celery. All of the above, none of the above. Everyone has a 'signature' bolognese, regardless of what is actually meant to go into a traditional version. It's the dish that any self-proclaimed non-chef can have a pop at and feel at ease with – even comforted by.

I have been asking people for their last meal on earth on my podcast, *Table Manners*, for three years now. We have heard too many 'Mum's roasts' and Christmas dinners to count, and, surprisingly, many people would choose to part with this world after a bowl of linguine vongole. But even more surprising to me was the lack of a lasagne or spaghetti bolognese, given that it seems to feature so prominently in so many of our childhood memories. British comedian Michael McIntyre is the only person who has said they would have a *homemade* spaghetti bolognese. It just isn't the same when you eat it in a restaurant; it is either too watery, under-seasoned, dry as a bone or drenched in too much sauce – it just doesn't taste like it does when someone close to you has made it. It is family in the form of a sauce.

* * *

'It's like pushing a watermelon out.' 'It's like shitting out a TV.' 'They wouldn't give me the epidural in time!' 'The epidural didn't work in time!' I was nervous about giving birth. In fact, I was absolutely terrified. I was the first of my friends to get pregnant and had visions of pain and horror, lovingly imparted by my mum, family members and friends' mums. And I had watched too many episodes of *One Born Every Minute*, a whistle-stop tour through everything that can possibly go wrong during labour.

When I found out I was pregnant, it was just after I had done a summer of festivals, so I had time (and money) on my hands to 'invest' in a Goop-style pregnancy. The prospect of sedation sounded rather inviting when it came to labour, and if I couldn't have that, then I wanted the next best thing.

The next best thing turned out to be an Ayurvedic doctor called Gowri Motha. Gowri was the first NHS obstetrician to introduce water births to the UK in the eighties. She's a pioneer in natural childbirth, encouraging women to prepare their bodies to enable the best chance of a 'gentle birth'. Even though Gowri is on a mission to make her methods a viable option within the NHS, accessible to all, she has become the Birkin bag of birthing, bringing her Ayurvedic practices to Kate Moss and Elle Macpherson, to name only two of her many celebrity clients. I initially went to her because my friend Quentin looked fantastic throughout her pregnancy and popped her baby out in four hours.

'I want what she's having,' I said and sought out the concoctor of Quentin's strange herbal teas. Perhaps Gowri could provide the miracle cure for a quick and pain-free birth. I adopted the gluten- and sugar-free (ish) diet encouraged by Dr Motha for months of my pregnancy, and lasagne was off the menu. I prepared for that first birth with such a ferocious focus that my husband, Sam, compared me to a Premier League footballer in training to win the Champions League. Sam saluted my efforts, joining me in eating millet bread for breakfast and buckwheat noodles for lunch, and even accepting the somewhat confusing rule against having mangoes in the house. My mother was less convinced; she was riled senseless each time I refused pudding at hers or sheepishly asked for the gluten-free option at a restaurant.

I ended up having a great, semi-gentle birth (if we omit the swearing and begging for drugs), which I like to put down to the time (and money) I invested in preparing for it. Aside from all the oils I rubbed onto my skin, all the pizzas and pastries I sacrificed and all the herbal teas and vitamins I militantly ingested morning and night, Gowri gave me an incredible confidence about giving birth, which outweighed my initial fear.

The second time around, I was a B-plus Gowri student; a tad arrogant and *laissez-faire*, thinking I knew how to jump through the hoops of pregnancy and birth while exhausted by a toddler. Sugar and carbs were my friend, particularly those Kingsland Road almond and chocolate croissants I would regularly pick up on the nursery run.

I had decided to have a baby at home this time, for reasons entirely unconnected to the fact that my mother-in-law had had two effortless births in a Brixton bathtub. She had always said that giving birth is 'like having a bit of a tummy ache'. Reader, it is not. I psychologically prepared by watching YouTube videos of Ricki Lake giving birth in her New York apartment, walking sideways up hills in Clissold Park and stomping around Victoria Park with my best mate Sarah – who was due two weeks after me. My baby was late, and Sarah looked ready to pop.

This was Sarah's first baby and you might say she had romanticised going into labour, just a little. Her husband Jamie was going to make a 'pregnancy ragu' as soon as she felt the rumblings of the baby knocking. It was to be an earthy distraction, calming and methodical. The sofrito would sweat, then the sauce would simmer for hours, the hob illuminating their dimly lit labour cave, Sarah clary-saged up to the eyeballs, Jamie gently mimicking the figure-of-eight movements with his hips while encouraging a regular lion's breath. I could picture Sarah on all fours, listening to Khruangbin, only to get up to stir the bolognese, the smells wafting in and out of her heavy breathing.

Sarah texted me throughout labour saying, 'This fucking hurts,' and eventually she gave birth to the angelic Casper to the sound of the Spice Girls. I'm not sure when the ragu got eaten or if she even fancied it by that point. I went to hold baby Casper at the hospital the next day, proud of my friend, jealous that I was still at the top of the diving board waiting to jump into a labour that was now two weeks overdue and starting to wonder about the powers of minced meat. Sam and I marched back from Homerton Hospital in the rain, me teetering on the edge of hysteria, determined to go into natural labour. I decided to make a bolognese.

I started it at 11 a.m., full of adrenaline and resentment towards our late arrival, certain that the tears in my eyes were not from the onions, adding pancetta and a bottle of red wine. It was going to sit there on the hob and I was going to sit on my birthing ball and together we would simmer with emotion and wait for the magic to happen. Miraculously, before a spoonful had passed my lips and over an episode of *Gilmore Girls,* I thought I could feel something.

I immediately texted Gowri unsure if this was simply another false alarm, or early labour. She told me to get to her North London clinic straight away and she would get the show on the road. And that she did – through the power of reflexology, some cranio-sacral therapy and a tired old Walkman playing high-frequency white noise in my ears (don't knock it till you've tried it). She sent me home two hours later, assuring me that the baby would arrive that evening. Sam was ordered to put the dust sheets down on the living-room floor, prepare the birthing pool and make sure the bolognese didn't stick to the bottom of the pan. I returned home with regular contractions deliciously rumbling inside me. The birthing team arrived, excited for us and ready to deliver this tardy babe. But then everything stopped: no more contractions, nothing. Maybe I was too excited and the baby got stage fright, who knows? The body and the mind are miraculous things during birth. The bolognese was sitting there, taunting me.

Exhausted from the ups and downs of the past eight hours, hungry and pissed off, I gave a simple instruction – 'Get the pasta on, Sam.' I think it was probably the best bolognese I have ever made, but there was no cause for celebration yet. I ate it miserably.

But an hour later, the game was back on. It was showtime. The ragu had worked! Four hours later, a perfect baby boy was in my hands, with his amniotic sack all over the sisal carpet (Sam hadn't checked to see if the dust sheets were waterproof). We sat all together with a cup of tea, a glass of champagne and chunks of chocolate, toasting his entrance. His middle name, Rafa, has the initials of each of the wonderful women who helped deliver him: Roisin, Aimee, Francine and Annie.

Was it sheer competitiveness on my part that did it? Was it that he was about to be two weeks overdue? Was it the power of Gowri? The four brilliant women's healing hands and words of encouragement or simply the magic of making that ragu? Who knows? But when I have another baby, I'll start with the sauce.

* * *

I bumped into my producer and friend Alice on our doorstep, dropping off a care package after my son had been born. She had filled a paper bag with a packet of spaghetti, fresh basil, a chunk of Parmesan, some dark chocolate and a big vat of homemade bolognese. She didn't ask to come in but cried as soon as she saw this tiny sleeping thing strapped to my chest. 'Sorry, I just can't help but cry at newborn babies,' she laughed through a joyful blub. I absolutely loved her for it.

* * *

Sam's father Pete's bolognese recipe is my favourite (perhaps because it's the quickest dish of his rather limited repertoire). I can see how much Sam loves making it; there is something he finds so satisfying about the chopping, the stirring, and the fact that the children prefer his to mine. When Sam was younger, Pete would announce to his wife and sons in the morning that he would be making dinner that evening. A hush would descend, broken only by the town bell ringing to mark this glorious and rare event.

It was always the same dish, the same recipe. Sam loved the taste of his dad's bolognese, but mostly he loved watching him make it. He would be back from school just in time to watch Pete make a start. Before any chopping had occurred, Pete would have struck up the CD player with jazz cascading out of it and poured a glass – or three – of red wine into one particular small goblet. Only *his* red wine goes into the goblet. It's slightly larger than a sherry glass and there's only one in the house, therefore the pouring of wine is rather free and regular.

Pete hums along, sips his wine and enjoys the steps to his spag bol. He makes his in a large frying pan, adding grated carrot, a beef Oxo cube and, right near the end, a large glug of wine so the alcohol is not fully burnt off. It's drier than I remember my mum's being, who left hers in a pressure cooker all day while she worked, so when we opened the door after returning from school, one sniff would tell us exactly what we were having for dinner. She served hers with the conchiglie shells, so the red water would sit in the shell like a rock pool, with the odd bit of mince swimming around.

We always return to Pete's recipe, even though it means I have to relinquish my conchiglie shells and my head-chef hat. It is worth it to watch Sam make it. He too will put jazz music on, have his bottle of wine ready and relive his dad's modest creation.

PETE'S SPAGHETTI BOLOGNESE

Olive oil
1 red onion, chopped
Garlic, chopped
500g mince
1 beef Oxo cube
1 tin of chopped tomatoes
Ground cinnamon
2 carrots, peeled
Salt and pepper
Red wine

1. *Put on some jazz (Bill Evans or Billie Holiday). Open a bottle of wine and pour yourself a glass.*
2. *Heat the olive oil in a large frying pan. Add the red onion and soften on a low heat for 10 minutes. Then add chopped garlic and cook for a minute.*
3. *Then the mince and the beef Oxo cube go in. Once the mince is fried off and no longer raw, add the tin of tomatoes. No purée!*
4. *Add a generous sprinkle of cinnamon and pour yourself another glass of wine.*
5. *Grate the carrots into the sauce and stir. Season to taste with black pepper and a small amount of salt.*
6. *Pour in some red wine at the end so you can really taste it.*

* * *

There is only one exception to the rule that spaghetti bolognese must be homemade, and that is when you are at International Café on Skopelos town's waterfront at 7 p.m. There is a low hum of mopeds, the air is thick and warm from the setting sun and smoking philosophers, the light is perfect and the town is slowly waking up from its siesta, ready for a night of handholding, citronella, gluttony and holiday spirit. International's Yanni greets you like family every year. It must be your first port of call when you set foot on Skopelos. You order his mother's meatballs in ouzo and a welcome Greek salad (something you will tire of after 14 days, but which is, at the first taste of feta smacked against vinegar and sweet tomatoes, glorious). Yanni's brother, Thasos, brings over a huge tray of drinks that are on the house: the largest glass of Greek rosé, a carafe for your mum who is always on her way and a Mythos for your husband. And the kids have the bolognese. It will be the only dish that they will eat for the next two weeks and you know it's the best bolognese on the island because after that fortnight of tasting, you are quite the connoisseur.

* * *

There is a taverna on Limnonari Beach on Skopelos where I would happily consume my last supper. Among olive groves and chirping crickets, you sit under linen canopies and pink and peach bougainvillea, taking in the lapping waves and the sound of children playing or mopeds coming down the hill. You listen closely to the ever-so-grumpy owner Vangelis's excellent jazz playlists, tasting fresh grilled octopus, fava-bean dip, mountain greens with feta and chilli, and the palest, most perfect tara-masalata, then feta with honey and filo and sesame seeds. I could go on. But while you eat all of these beautiful dishes, you will be ducking and diving to get away from the wasps. Taking a rushed bite of your seafood spaghetti, you will simultaneously inhale smoke from the mound of burning coffee on your table – a deterrent to scare the pests away. You will finish the meal within minutes with an added side of heartburn. That meal will include spaghetti bolognese for the children, of course. Spaghetti bolognese is, inevitably, a wasp's personal favourite. There is no rhyme or reason as to why most years there are so many wasps on Skopelos, then another year there will be virtually none, but it will be the main point of conversation throughout the meal.

The name of Vangelis's taverna is Lemonis. One year I got stung by a wasp – on a non-wasp year, ironically – and he told me that the best remedy for a sting was very hot water dabbed on the area. 'You will cry from the heat, but it will get the poison out. Dab MORE. LONGER. Do it!' It only took me thirty years of wasp stings to attain this simple recommendation. I share it with you happily, because it really does take away the sting much quicker, leaving you with a manageable itch.

Our good friend, William McDonald is the most charming gentleman you will ever meet, and he has an incredible knack of keeping your wine glass full throughout the night. My mother and William get along extraordinarily. William's husband, Chris Sweeney, has been coming to Skopelos with his family for as long as us – thirty years. We have shared many meals, drinks, laughter, Wasp-Eze, and tears together as the Wares and the Sweeneys. We have shared pasta on their balcony, cheese and ham toasties by the pool, and first White Russians on first drunk nights. Chris has always been – aside from the time he split my eyelid open dunking me in the pool – a gentle older sibling to me.

Chris married William on Skopelos the year after Sam and I tied the knot there. Their wedding was totally different to ours: different locations, different vows, different guests, different food, different music. Far more chic, but just as fun.

Straight after Chris and Will's wedding ceremony, the wasps were *angry*. Perhaps they were sick of the throngs of jubilant people joining them in the most picturesque spot on the island: a rock with one lowly tree, capturing the brilliant sunset in all its glory. Perhaps the fanning of our joyful tears pissed them off. But as we climbed off the rock to leave the treacherous spot and headed to the harbour to catch the reception boat and toast the happy couple, Sam was seen by all standing on a jagged rock, pulling his pants down. The wedding party looked on as Sam, his toned, godly body lit by the golden glow of the setting sun, as poised and tense as a mythical statue, tried to tend to the sting on his bottom. I have been told that this was a high point of the wedding for many of the guests, outshining the rendition of Whitney Houston's 'Step by Step' I sang as a duet with Will Young later that evening.

Tooth

Teeth

M y sister knocked my front tooth out when I was seven. It happened during an over-tired bath time, when a few pesky splashes aimed at my sister ended in her grabbing my head and persistently banging my face against the side of the bath. I watched my newly grown tooth crumbling into the muggy bath water. My mum fished around with a sieve to try to salvage what was left of the disintegrated tooth, but it was no use; the shards swam among the suds and were lost. But it was okay because it meant I could go and see my dentist, Dr Charles Ferber, to have a new tooth fitted. Hello, Charlie, if you're reading this (which I know you will be, as Mum will have bought you a copy). The replacement tooth was a cement-like putty that would supposedly serve me well until my older years. It looked so realistic I didn't end up getting a proper veneer until my twenties.

I've never understood people's fear of the dentist. I longed for my Wimpole Street appointments where I would be greeted like a long-lost niece, with a two-hand cupping of my face and a kiss on both chubby cheeks. It was whiffs of sweet mint and wealthy women's perfume and flicking through magazines in the waiting room on a school day. My mum was from a working-class family, always a staunch Labour supporter and NHS lover, so we never had private health care – never really believed in it – but when it came to teeth, Mum always sent us to central London. It is a contradiction that I broached with my mum recently. She explained that my grandma had lost all her back teeth when she was twenty-six – 'because of the Blitz and nerves' – so she had always taken my mum to private dental practices ever since she was a little girl. My grandma was obsessed with 'good teeth', so I guess my mum inherited that trait, the irony being that Mum is at the dentist as regularly as the supermarket due to a relentless list of complications surrounding her molars, her crowns, root canals . . . you name it, she's had the problem and a procedure to fix it.

* * *

One Saturday evening in Streatham, my new tooth came out with a bite of a toffee apple. I was fourteen and this was the first time it happened, but it would not be the last. The toffee had ripped out the cement that held my replacement tooth in place and as I looked in the mirror at my friend Amber's house, I realised I was somewhat toothless once again. I'd have remained happy in that state until a trip back to Charlie the following week, but I was meant to be singing at a competition in Blackheath the next day. It was going to be in front of an audience of girls my age and a string of judges, and my singing teacher had cajoled me into doing it with significant support from my mother. I was in a state of deep dread already. I was never good at performing in front of people; my eyes would hit the ground, my feet would awkwardly pull inwards and a sniffle would emerge mid belt. But I always got a decent song in the end-of-year show, and I was never short of pushy mothers, friends and teachers who seemed to believe in my voice more than I did.

So being toothless on a Saturday night in Streatham suited me just fine. I assumed I wouldn't have to go to the competition. No need to anxiously wait in line, no need to sing 'The Man I Love' or 'Someone to Watch Over Me', no need to watch the prize go to a terrifyingly confident fourteen-year-old with a buxom breast behind a conservative black dress, whose recital of Gilbert and Sullivan's 'Alone, and Yet Alive' made her look like she was ready to open the first night at the Royal Opera House.

But my mother, as ever, had other plans. Sunday morning, there I was at Christ the King College in Blackheath, waiting for my turn to sing, with a dodgy-looking 'tooth' made of temporary grey putty, cemented on by an out-of-hours emergency dentist. Unsurprisingly, I sang with my head even further down, reluctant to open my mouth to reveal my protruding putty tooth. The winner of the 'Song from a Musical' group was a young auburn-haired starlet called Florence Welch. She sang the 'Theme from *Mahogany* (Do You Know Where You're Going To)' quite brilliantly.

* * *

Sam and I met at Honeywell Primary School in Wandsworth, but we ran into each other again in 2001 at Movement, a drum-and-bass night in Brixton's old St Matthew's Church. It had been turned into a nightclub called, inevitably, Mass. It was the place Amber and I would go every month, getting the Number 37 bus from my house. I would be dressed head to toe in black (to hide the sweat), trainers and big Claire's hoops, with a spare pair in my miniature black PVC rucksack for when I lost one in the rave; Amber would be in a pink H&M racer-back mesh vest and jeans – both of us with slicked-back pony tails. We had £5 fake IDs, which worked every time and were, indeed, the best £5 we ever spent. We'd walk up the dingy, winding staircase as the sound of the impending bass crept louder and louder with each step, about to set foot in a place of total safety and joy. All we did was dance together, Amber and I.

Our constant companion (or absent friend) was revealed under the fluorescent UV lights. My 'rave tooth' would pull a laugh here and there as I would look toothless whenever I smiled under the UV. It made the fake part of my front tooth invisible, so that everyone could see the results of my sister's nifty work: the remnants of my jagged front peg in all its glory.

The night I spotted Sam, it was a quick glance and a nod on the dance floor, an acknowledgement of each other; we were too busy dancing to flirt just yet. That would happen two years later on Streatham High Road at the Butterfly Bar. I got to our mate's drum-and-bass night, Potent Soundz, extra early one Christmas Eve to watch Sam play the warm-up set. I bought his older brother Joe an agenda-filled beer so he would report back to Sam that I was 'safe' and he should ask me out. Sam and I flirted ever so slightly – a quick touch of the shoulder, a look in the eye or the offer of a Southern Comfort and lemonade. That night lit a little spark, and by Boxing Day we were texting back and forth from our Nokia phones, while I sat in the back of my mum's Renault Mégane on my way to Kempton Park Races for our family tradition. The texts weren't exactly flirtatious – instead polite and enthusiastic – but I felt special that he was happy to use his phone credit on me, and he kept replying with a question. Drum and bass was at the heart of our reconnection, music a stirring beat to our relationship.

Sam and I decided to go to Fabric together one Thursday night to see the DJ Andy C play a set. I was designated driver – saving up for a trip to South America – and Sam never took his Kingston

College hours too seriously, so off we drove to Farringdon in my trusty spearmint-coloured Cinquecento.

Six months in to our relationship, going to mid-week d'n'b nights together felt like the norm to us, but it was still exciting and ambitious for a date. We were still trying to impress each other, still understanding each other. It was all new yet familiar, and I already knew I loved him. While watching the godlike DJ on his plinth, we cheered, danced, sweated and kissed. But when the DJ pulled up a tune for a rewind, out came Sam's trigger finger, and with an over-emphatic 'Blup!' it met the end of my glass Coca-Cola bottle and knocked the tooth straight out again. I turned to him and his mouth dropped. Over the sound system I cheerily shouted, 'Oh, don't worry about it, it's not real anyway,' trying not to smile too widely, secretly mortified that this was the way my future husband would discover I no longer owned a front left tooth. We left the tooth on the sticky floor and kept on dancing, and laughing, lost in the treble and bass of the night. Once in a blue moon we still go raving, but I never ate another toffee apple again.

Shellfish

I remember my mum and dad being invited by neighbours down the road to their annual oyster, Guinness and champagne night. My mum always returned hungry, disgruntled and lambasting the ritual. To me, it sounded like the very image of sophistication. To be an adult. To be eating shellfish.

* * *

My first taste of an oyster was at the OXO Tower on the South Bank. It seemed to be *the* place to go, the red 'OXO' sign a beacon of exclusivity as you crossed over Blackfriars Bridge. The only way I was going to get to the top floor was if my mum was paying. It was Mother's Day sometime in the late nineties – I must have been fourteen or fifteen. There was a set menu with the offering of an 'oyster in a neon green jelly' for starters and I was sure that by now I was old enough to appreciate them. So I ordered the oyster, nervous, excited and concerned that I had gone for the smallest starter on the menu. It arrived in its shell, surrounded by dots of green-apple slime that didn't look ample enough to mask the taste of the ocean. I was squeamish about the idea of the raw oyster still being alive and had been told you weren't meant to chew them – apparently a *huge* faux pas. People talk about the ritual of eating an oyster as they would talk about enjoying a fine wine; the oyster liquor, the 'sweetness and brininess of the bivalves'. In my head I was Ursula, the sea witch in *The Little Mermaid*, devouring a poor unfortunate soul. This strange anticipation was like waiting for Rameses Revenge at Chessington: you didn't want to be sick, but you couldn't back out now. I closed my eyes, tipped my head back, swallowed the thing whole and was instantly reminded of salty snot dripping down my throat.

* * *

I never give up on any kind of food – mainly because I am greedy – so I tried oysters again in my twenties. I was a waitress for a catering firm serving up canapés and luxury artisanal titbits at fashion events and magazine parties. We were all just trying to make a bit of money in between university holidays and perhaps weren't as passionate about small bowls as the owners felt we should be. I'd wince when one of us was shouted at but suffered through it for the culinary opportunities. It was in the back corridors of Kensington Palace that I had my first taste of deep-fried sage, pata negra and foie gras. I would shove morsels in my mouth before returning to fill up my serving plate for another lap of the room. At one particularly luxurious event there was an old-school oyster cart, with a lovely elderly shucker who told me that the way to eat an oyster was to massage the raw oyster by pushing it up to the roof of your mouth and letting it stay there a while before swallowing. This made more sense to me; why would you want something seemingly so delicate, exotic and special to disappear so quickly? Unfortunately, oysters weren't as easy to conceal on the floor as an asparagus spear dusted in bottarga, so I never got to practice that particular method.

How to Shuck an Oyster

Take it in your left hand (or right if you're left-handed). With the core of the oyster by your wrist, point the knife away from you and edge the knife, bit by bit, around the opening of the oyster. Go all the way around, edging inside the shell a little more every time. You'll feel a little click as it releases. It may take some time. It may feel like a lifetime. It will happen. Open up the oyster and try not to let any flakes fall into the watery centre.

At least, I think that's how you shuck one.

* * *

A decade into our relationship, Sam and I were on a night away in Whitstable and it was my mission to right my indifference towards the enigmatic aphrodisiac that is the oyster. Twenty-something and on a budget, we stayed at an inexpensive B&B, recommended by my friend Samantha, who had just had a dirty weekend away there. I was ready to introduce Sam to a night of shellfish, sophistication and *amour*. A topless man with a generous gut opened the door, revealed he was 'cleaning out the hot tub for ya' and took us to a room bathed in the smell of Febreze and disinfectant. He gestured towards a rickety four-poster bed covered in plastic flowers, then asked how we wanted our eggs in the morning. When he immediately answered his own question with 'Fertilised?' I felt somewhat less lascivious. Samantha later asked if I suspected it was a swingers' hotel due to the sound of feet running up and down the stairs all night.

Always one for a theme, we started our evening at Wheelers Oyster Bar, a 156-year-old fish institution with the front painted in baby pink – enticing and gentle to the wandering, and perhaps apprehensive, oyster eater. A deep-fried oyster was an option, a perfect entry point for Sam, who dreaded eating the sea. Four oysters arrived drenched in garlicy, glossy batter and surrounded by limp salad leaves. Although they were now certainly not alive, there was a milkiness when biting down into them that didn't sit well with us. Sam stopped his oyster journey before it had begun, while I ploughed through three raw ones drowned in shallot vinaigrette. Perhaps with a spark of lust, I had completed my first challenge of somewhat enjoying it.

We went to a bistro for our main meal and, being a grown woman on a romantic night out, I ordered the lobster. Sam sat across from me with his bowl of risotto, a look of disgust across his face as I hacked into the legs of the poor creature. Chatting away while sucking a claw, I tried to disguise how I was struggling with the bastard, but it became achingly clear when I pelted a load of lobster juice at the woman sitting beside me. Unbeknown to her, a bit of meat-flecked bisque was perched on the right shoulder of her black silk shirt. Luckily none of her eating party had noticed in the dimly lit bistro. It was the ultimate *Pretty Woman* moment: I was Julia Roberts flinging her snail across the room. If I hadn't been worried about the lady cottoning on to the fact that sea juice was seeping through her shirt, I would have chirped, 'Slippery little suckers!' Instead, I ordered the bill straight away and we made a run for it. Sam never got pudding, successfully avoided a fertilised egg and is always suspicious of a crab or lobster on the menu nowadays. His loss.

* * *

My friend Liz grew up in Australia, and at ten years of age you would find her and her brother going down to Harrington, near Port Macquarie, seeking out oysters planted on the rocks. They would spot them on a wall separating the open ocean from the lagoon, and she would shuck them with her short fat knife, a lemon in the other hand, ready to feast on them, until she would get belly ache from devouring so many in one sitting. She would have grazes on her legs and often bleeding feet from oyster-shell cuts. On other days she would dance the twist in the sand to find pippies (the Australian version of a cockle) and take them back home and boil them in a large pot with ocean water. Other tricks included putting minced meat in a pair of stockings and dangling them off a dam to entice crabs, or 'yabbies' as they call them. Her childhood sounded adventurous and wholesome, and the opposite of mine when it came to eating fish. Mine was either boil-in-the-bag cod with parsley sauce or, at any Jewish function, smoked fish and herring. Post COVID lockdown 1, Liz and I went to Tom Brown's Cornerstone in Hackney Wick on a balmy night to celebrate a light version of freedom after a long few months indoors. We sat and drank orange wine and hung onto each other's words, ramming all our news into our two-hour allocated sitting. An oyster came out with the main man, Chef Tom bringing it to our table. It was a pickled oyster. Just the thought of it made the corner of my mouth curl up to my squinting eye. I wasn't sure how to handle this one. While I pondered, Liz had already popped hers in her mouth and chewed, looking at me, confused, as I attempted to 'massage' it in the roof of my mouth.

'Whaddya doing? Just bite it,' she laughed.

I did as I was told and it was a totally new experience; I tasted the sweetness, the right ventricle, the left, no grit, just a tart taste of the ocean – and I enjoyed it. I wanted to have another.

* * *

Five summers after Sam's stung bottom, we revisited the crime scene with not a wasp or an ashtray of smoking coffee in sight.

We couldn't quite believe it, given the time of year, but apparently it had been a wet April in Skopelos and when the wasps are underground they get drowned by the rain. The happy couple, William and Chris, joined Mum, Sam, our two kids and my brother Alex for an early supper to celebrate William's birthday. We sat down at Korali Taverna on the water's edge of Agnondas, while the Greeks were just getting to the beach for a swim. Having two young children means I cannot flirt with the relaxed time schedule of breakfast after noon and dinner from 10.30 p.m. I am delighted about that.

When I saw 'sea urchin with orzo' on the menu, I was like a kitten waiting to be stroked. It had to be ordered. For the book, of course.

No one at the table wanted it; everyone said they wouldn't taste it. I retorted with, 'Everyone in LA loves it!' People who eat sea urchin are part of the same club as people who order oysters. They speak in the same language; they can't just semi-like a sea urchin, they 'loooooooove uni'. And they will always smugly call it uni – part of the remit to be in this seafood set. *Uni* is the Japanese word for a sea urchin's sex glands, and apparently it is a world-class delicacy. And, lo and behold, an aphrodisiac, just like its lusty playmate, the oyster. I'd always avoided it during omakase dinners at my favourite place to eat Sushi in Los Angeles, the legendary Sushi Park. *Omakase* is 'I'll leave it up to you' in Japanese, but my friend Benny told me that you could state what you weren't up for eating at the beginning of the meal, before you left it up to the chef to choose. Uni was the one dish I put on my list. But look at me now.

The plate arrived bearing small terracotta-coloured pieces that looked like my daughter's rolled-up Play-Doh remnants, interspersed with lemony orzo. It didn't look how I had seen it, and avoided it, in Japanese restaurants: delicate and soft, with a surface of erect taste-bud-like fur and a strong resemblance to a cut-out tongue.

'Guys, you can't have an opinion on something unless you have tried it,' I said, remembering the last time I had said this was that very lunchtime to my daughter, who wouldn't touch a beautiful, sweet Greek tomato. The birthday boy shook his head and winced, knowing he was next to try the dish. Mum crossed her arms defiantly and my brother told me to 'stop going on about the book'. They all watched across the table like the celebrity waiting their turn in the Bushtucker Trial.

It wasn't delicious on the first bite, nor on the second or even the third. It was soft, yet you felt your teeth breaking and intruding on the surface, exactly how you would imagine biting through a tongue or a gland. I had three mouthfuls, just enough to prove I could have an opinion. And that opinion is that I never wish to order it again.

Omakase.

* * *

My sister Hannah likes to be among beautiful things: in her house, in what she wears, where she lives and certainly where she will eat. She has an effortless elegance and eccentricity to her style; she always has. When she first moved to Los Angeles, she would take me to a hidden Italian restaurant set in the valley of Laurel Canyon, where Joni Mitchell used to frequent – a beacon of old Californian bohemia – where lava lamps bubble and you still feel there is the possibility of free love and an acoustic guitar popping out at any given moment. You'd eat a rustic selection of Italian food to the sound of psychedelia and romantic chit-chat, the lighting a warm glow flattering the faces of each dining guest. Yet she will still shine the brightest among all of them, because she is the most perfectly beautiful of all. Or, on another occasion, she would demand that we go for early Dirty Martinis and oysters at Sunset Tower, getting the best table because she's charmed the front of house with her inviting British accent and a dazzling slip dress she just flung on, her hair still wet because she's *always* late to any gathering.

She would give me the best seat at the table, so I could watch Sean Penn saunter past to his seat. She'd seen them all there before. And they had certainly already glanced over to her. She would instruct me on how to enjoy a Dirty Martini, demanding the waiter make it 'filthy' with a wink and extra brine. It suits her, the glamour of the setting and the order of oysters, the very pinnacle of sophistication. The circular table, the white table cloth with the grand silver platter of oval pearly shells sitting in the middle, complimenting her piercing green-grey eyes. The tiny spoon placed in the pretty silver bowl full of vinaigrette and that punch of bright yellow from the lemon peel. Her table is a still-life of excitement, enchantment and allure, my sister the embodiment of a twenty-first-century Botticelli among her sea shells.

How to Eat an Oyster

Although the oyster has not yet awakened my 'spiritual taste buds' like it did for the formidable oyster eater and writer M.F.K. Fisher, I have learnt what works best for me.

And because my greatest oyster experience was at Tom Brown's Cornerstone, I thought I would take my lead from the man himself who, after one conversation, has taught me so much about them. Here is what I learnt:

- *One oyster will filter around 55 litres of water a day, so where they come from makes a huge difference to how they will taste and the size and texture of them as they take in their surroundings and different minerals.*

- *The oyster that I ate at his restaurant was a Carlingford oyster from Ireland. Upstream from where they grow is a big pine forest and they grow in slow-moving water, meaning you not only get a nuttiness to their taste, but they have large barnacles and grow big and meaty.*
- *Never swallow. Innuendos aside, if you chew it and savour it, you get the flavour, the meatiness, the creaminess and the sweetness. When you swallow an oyster, you get nothing out of its story, and it's like having a paracetamol.*
- *Try a Pacific oyster with green tabasco and a cold beer.*
- *On a good native oyster, cracked black pepper will give it a purer flavour.*
- *If you find yourself in Mexico, try them with salsa picante and a generous squeeze of lime.*

I will also add in here a suggestion given to me by a friend, which Chef Tom thought sounded inviting:

- *Pour a shot of vodka over the oyster while it's still in its shell, then chew and swallow the sucker along with the alcohol. It may numb the fear for a novice.*

White Bread

My dear schoolfriend Alice would always let me have the first pour of the blue-top milk over my cereal when I stayed at hers. I would sneak a lick of the foil top where the cream had formed while the fridge door was open. Not only did Alice have full-fat milk, but her mum always made sure they had the heftiest loaf of white tin bread to feed her and her four hungry siblings. It's funny because, although we were the house with a cupboard full of treats and snacks, our kitchen was also full of Vogel's bread, semi-skimmed – or even worse – the 1-per-cent-fat orange-top milk that was essentially murky water, Müllerlights, o-per-cent-fat cottage cheese, Just Right cereal and Olivio spread: nothing was full of fat in our fridge. Mum and I were always consciously watching our weight, due to our insatiable appetites and adoration of food. We never had thick, fluffy, mineral-white loaves of bread; that was saved for outings to the local Italian restaurant or when I stepped through Alice's door. Her house had two distinctive smells: toast in the morning or Lapsang souchong in the afternoon. Her mum would make a pot of two scoops Assam, three scoops

Lapsang, and it would fill the room with smoke and warmth. The scent of that Brockley house was so distinctive, with its perfect synergy of comfort, Bohemia and grandeur.

After a party in south-east London, the secondary-school trio Amber, Alice and I would sit at Alice's kitchen table late into the night, giving a debrief on the evening in hushed voices over a cup of sweet Yorkshire Tea and two slices of butter and Marmite toast – sustenance after a lengthy night of dancing to EZ, Sweet Female Attitude and So Solid Crew. 'What did Matt mean when he said, "You're my best friend," but then later came to dance with me?' 'Did you see Jack doing a dance-off with Roxanne?' 'Who played the best set?' We weren't badly behaved teenagers; in fact, we were rather innocent, so the end-of-night tea and toast, the unadulterated pleasure of butter on bread, was like toasting to friendship, sorority and teenage confessions with champagne, burning through slices and stories.

At thirty-five, I now live round the corner from Alice's family house in Brockley, with a family of my own. Alice has her baby girl and lives opposite her parents, so we meet up at the top of Telegraph Hill with her carrying little Nancy in a sling. The first question I ask is still, 'How was last night?' Nowadays our conversations centre around sleep routines and regressions (Nancy's finally sleeping two and a half hours solidly and Al feels like a new woman), television, podcasts and family. As we walked down Evelina Road in Nunhead on one of our recent walks, we passed Ayres, a family bakery that has been there since the 1950s. 'Oh, that's where Mum used to get that white bread you always liked at ours, Jess,' Alice said. Immediately, I marched in, bought a large white tin loaf and took it back to my house for a doorstop of Marmite and butter on toast. I was fifteen again and it tasted just as good as I remembered. 'It's very moving that you've come back home to that loaf,' Alice texted me, after I had sent a picture of me with a chunk of buttered bread and a huge smile. Now I'm just waiting on the right teapot to start on the Lapsang/Assam mix. Once I have it, I expect I will finally feel like an adult.

* * *

I always wanted school dinners at Honeywell Primary. I wanted the waiting in line, the weekly variety of lunch, the daily 'hello' to the dinner ladies, knowing I would be a satisfied customer. I would have relished a two-course meal made up of guaranteed stodge, and that beautiful finale: the choice between a warm but weak chocolate sponge cake with equally un-chocolatey chocolate custard or the shortbread biscuit with raspberry yoghurt poured over it. However, my family knew my appetite all too well and so I was confined to bringing in a packed lunch. A sandwich, over which I glared at the hot meals with a jealous stomach.

I would sit with my regular group at lunch: Zoe Pilger, Nancy Griffin and Christina Ashford. Zoe was the leader of the group, Nancy was the naughty one and Christina was the quietest. Nancy was the only school dinners girl out of us four and she didn't have much interest in the food, which suited me perfectly. Each would inspect the other's box or plate, beady-eyed and interested. Zoe usually ate a war-time corned beef and pickle sandwich and I ate a flat and leaky tuna mayonnaise, bulldozed by the weight of an apple. Christina would have a pristine ham and cheese sandwich, which was all I ever really wanted, but Mum wouldn't allow ham in the house. The closest I got to it was Bernard Matthews' wafer-thin turkey ham, which was so sad and wet that your bread would be sodden by the time you went to eat it. Other days it was Zoe unashamedly sucking on a chicken drumstick, flinging the bone around as she gesturally told us a story, while I tucked in to cold chicken nuggets that gave me hiccups as I inhaled them so quickly. In the summer months, a frozen water bottle of Vimto would have bruised a perfect peach or squashed my cottage cheese and Marmite sandwich on brown bread. It was always a good day if I discovered chicken liver pâté in a Warburtons milk roll, a Walnut Whip or a shop-bought prawn mayonnaise in my lunchbox. Even if I didn't like my packed lunch, I would savour ever mouthful, even polishing off Nancy's discarded dinners while we swapped *Baby-Sitters Club* books and gossiped about boys. All the while, Sam Burrows would be in an Eagles T-shirt at the end of the trellis table, mumbling to his strictly boys' club, eating a peanut butter and jam sandwich. Neither of us knew that he would become my husband twenty-five years later, and that we would be serving exactly the same sandwich to our future children.

* * *

By Year Six, I'd had my first taste of 'dining out' with Zoe, Nancy and Christina. Every Tuesday after school we would set off to a greasy spoon down the road and each have a buttery slice of toast and a sweet tea for £1 before heading off to an after-school art class. We felt so self-sufficient, strutting down to the café where we would be met by the warm Greek-Cypriot owner, who would ask, 'The usual?' Capital Gold would play and we would giggle over our strong tea, over-sweet by our lengthy tilt of the sugar pourer.

At twelve or thirteen, Year Eight, when we had all separated to different schools, I would get the 137 bus to King's Road and meet up with Nancy for a coffee on a Saturday afternoon. Nancy didn't live around Chelsea, far from it, but she was always at the King's Road Caffè Nero, smoking Marlboro Lights, commanding an audience, latte after latte. She would stay there for hours cackling, smoking, flirting or frightening young boys who were enthralled by her confidence. If I stayed over at her Battersea house, her mum would make us steak minute with creamy mushroom sauce while she fed her younger two children baked beans and pasta. We would fall asleep in Nancy's attic room to the sound of the trains on the track at the back of the garden on their way to Clapham Junction or Victoria.

We drifted apart for a while, but Nancy went on to have three kids, and later became a nurse at a hospice where her Uncle Cliff passed away in 1996. I remember going to her eleventh birthday party in the gardens of the hospice, just so Uncle Cliff could celebrate it with her and her family.

Zoe and I would go for a tuna sweetcorn or chicken and bacon mayo baked potato at Jackets on Clapham High Street, but by 1999, when a shiny new Starbucks opened on Abbeville Road – one of ten in London – Jackets was a distant memory. Zoe would have a cappuccino, because she was always that much more mature, and I would stick with a mocha, but I distinctly remember discovering that milk doesn't go well with their Tazo green tea. We danced between Café Rouge thin fries and our mums' home-cooked meals or Vegemite on toast at Zoe's dad's place down the road.

Although Christina and I went to the same secondary school, we haven't kept up with each other's lives, but I did see her in a Brixton Sainsbury's car park once, proudly pregnant.

It doesn't matter if we've lost contact, how long I haven't spoken to them, or how much time apart there has been between us, when I smell butter on ever-so-slightly burnt toast, we're suddenly all eleven again.

* * *

I met my best friend Sarah in October 2004 at Sussex University's Lewes Court halls. I had not been at university long, and most weekends I had driven back home to London to see Sam, determined to make our long-distance relationship work. It felt disloyal diving head-first into Freshers' Week, which seemed to me to be just a lot of drinking cider and blackcurrant, aimless pub crawls and people auditioning for friendships. And I missed Sam. I didn't want him to think I had outgrown him by staying away. So I invited him down to meet my new 'friends' at a Halloween party, where I met Sarah.

Sam managed to get so drunk (later he confessed it was an extreme case of Dutch courage) that we missed most of the party and I ended the evening helping him vomit in the grass outside my dorm window. While I carted this six-foot-two drunken weight away from the party through the fluorescently lit, smoke-filled corridors, I remember seeing a curly-haired six-foot beauty dressed in baggy Carhartt jeans, Converse high-tops and a hoodie languidly leaning against the wall. This was Sarah. I loudly spewed out some frivolous chit-chat – one of my specialities during university – and left the party behind, resenting Sam's arrival on campus.

* * *

On paper, my friendship with Sarah shouldn't have worked. I was a seemingly confident, brash South Londoner, keen to please, and I wore Uggs. She was quiet, cutting, highly intelligent, wore Jordans and was an Arsenal fan. But we bonded through music, family, not being accomplished drinkers (though we gave it a good shot) and, most importantly, through beige food. That first year saw our student loans go on Anchor butter, economy sliced white bread and Danish bacon from the tuck shop on campus. We would smoke weed and eat too many salted Doritos until the corners of our mouths bled, then have bacon sandwiches and live out the cliché of every twentysomething: discussing *Before Sunrise* and *Before Sunset* at length. By the end of the year I had gained a stone, added Fiona Apple, Regina Spektor, Amp Fiddler and Pearl Jam to my playlists and bought a pair of high-tops.

We decided to live together in the final year of university, along with our friends Chabbi and Felix (aka Fe), in an apartment on the Western Road towards Hove, above an independent art gallery. Fe was hardly there as his band, The Maccabees, were starting to do well and he was touring most of the time, so it was mainly Sarah, Chabbi and me. Soon enough it was confirmed that we were all as slobbish as each other, with bins overspilling, a horrendous fly infestation and endless dust. This didn't stop me cooking over-spiced tagines and offering up a mid-week Eton Mess or a trifle to flatmates who were probably happier with a Golden Grill shish kebab from down the road. Sarah and I were inseparable; we would talk each other to sleep, putting the world to rights in my double bed when our boyfriends weren't staying over. It was the great romance of my life at that moment, and it was building to a simmering tension.

We knew each other so well that every word *unsaid* was a loaded gun. We were constantly breaking up, without uttering a word to each other, only to make the reunion that much more heated and emotional. The intensity of our relationship made the highs and lows addictive and destructive. I would creep around like a guilty party, accepting complicity to a crime I wasn't even sure of committing. I would deliberate with Sam about what I had done to upset her; Sam would shrug and nonchalantly call her my girlfriend. Even though I laughed it off, there was a certain intensity to our friendship that was more dramatic, brutal, eye-opening and all-consuming than anything Sam and I were used to. We got through the rest of the year in Brighton stoically and vowed to never live together again.

* * *

By 2011 we were living together again nonetheless – with Sarah's twin sister Samantha, Sam and our friend Jason included – on Dalberg Road, Brixton. I was now a signed artist, Sarah was working as a booker at an East London club called Cargo, Sam was a teaching assistant and Samantha was in advertising. We would go out to Corsica Studios and Fabric, eat at the indoor market, have Saturday-night *X Factor* dinners and poker nights and be the home of any after-party sleepover. It was fun and we were ever-so-slightly more mature than we had been as students. That is, until 5 October 2011, when we were at our friend's wedding and a drunken fight with a trifle ensued. Friends had been asked to make puddings and I had offered up my mum's trifle – an absolute beauty. However, I can confirm that among a sea of cupcakes, cookies, Victoria sponges and brownies, a trifle does not fare well and will always be the bridesmaid. So at the end of the night, there I was with my housemates, drunkenly holding my mother's borrowed glass bowl of untouched trifle on Lavender Hill. I believe Sarah threw the first punch with a smearing of whipped cream and custard on my face. I returned this with a raspberry sponge and then there was an actual smack to my face. We were eventually broken up, travelled home in separate cars and didn't speak to each other for a week. The following Monday, when I was in my friend Kid Harpoon's Highbury flat, we wrote a song called 'Wildest Moments' about the incident. And it makes sense that it's about Sarah. My high and my low, my right and my wrong, my cherished pain in the backside. And I guess the slapping of my mum's trifle in the face isn't the worst way to end a night.

MUM'S TRIFLE

Food writer Grace Dent spooned this trifle into her mouth while standing up, cooing over the perfect ratio of whipped cream to hardened custard and Swiss roll. I can attest that it deserves all the respect it gets.

Bird's custard powder
Milk
Swiss roll (raspberry)
Tinned raspberries
Sherry (optional)
Whipping cream
Almonds (toasted or untoasted) or Hundreds and
Thousands

1. *Prepare the custard as it says on the packet.*
2. *Slice the Swiss roll and lay the slices at the bottom of a glass bowl. Pour over the tinned raspberries (and add the sherry if desired).*
3. *Pour over the custard and leave it to solidify a little – this is the special thing about my mother's trifle. If it's winter, put it in the garden or on a windowsill for an hour.*
4. *When the custard is set, whip the cream and spoon it over the custard.*
5. *Add the almonds or sprinkles.*

* * *

I don't live with Sarah any more, and we've moved on from 25p slices of Marmite toast to £4.50 sourdough loaves from the Dusty Knuckle Bakery in Dalston. I make the trip to Hackney to see my best friend, but also so I can wait for a Dusty Knuckle porchetta sandwich with quince aioli, crisp dressed lettuce leaves and fresh focaccia. It is like the very best friendships: complex, intense, generous and absolutely essential.

Toast

Like everyone else, I tried making a sourdough starter in lockdown. I ceremoniously called it 'Captain Sir Tom Moore' after the 100-year-old veteran who walked laps and laps of his garden to raise money for NHS workers. Sadly, that starter was a non-starter and I instantly regretted the name. Then Sarah's husband Jamie gave me a bit of his, 'Mario', a thriving firecracker of fermentation that gave birth to my newly named sourdough son 'Luigi'. The naming was far more fun than the actual making, especially when you realise that the temporary mini oven you're currently using doesn't fit the loaf. After one trip to my neighbour's house to borrow their kitchen, I concluded that breadmaking was too heavy a burden and settled for the bakery down the road. But at no point did I forego a slice of toast.

I was promised a piece of buttered toast in hospital after giving birth the first time. It never came and I wouldn't have been able to stomach it anyway, but I have never forgotten that missed slice. Then there's my dad's ritual of spreading marmalade on cold dense brown toast every morning. Or Ayres Bakery's white tin loaf or their other offering, the levain five-grain. Or challah bread that burns at the sides, which only intensifies the sweetness of the loaf, or, even sweeter, challah French toast for breakfast.

Bread is a wonder, waiting for the perfect partner, so below are my mere – yet mighty – suggestions of how to pep up a simple slice of toast.

TOAST WITH MARMITE, PEANUT BUTTER AND CHEESE

This means teenage nights back at Jack Peñate's after a house party. Alice was Jack's girlfriend by now and I would sit and debrief Jack's mum, Clare, while he noodled on his guitar in the background. Clare would host us round her kitchen table in the low light, in a chinoiserie kimono, Marlboro Light in hand, with the other hand tapping two tablets of Canderel sweetener into our cups of piping-hot tea. To my knowledge, she is the only person who still uses Canderel. Clare, along with the fiercely loyal Alice, would kindly indulge my delusion that there was romance in the air between me and Matt Weeks (a school friend I was mad about at the time). It was an unrequited romance, but they would conjure up potential in each missed moment, each misleading 'you're my best friend'. There was comfort in the smell of that fag smoke and the tap of the Canderel.

With the cup of tea came a humble and excellent discovery, which, alongside her glamour and storytelling, will forever immortalise Clare as someone with great taste (and taste buds): her Marmite on toast:

2 slices of bread
Butter

Marmite
Crunchy peanut butter
Cheddar cheese

1. *Toast the bread.*
2. *Spread butter on the toast.*
3. *Spread Marmite on the toast.*
4. *Add a generous slap of crunchy peanut butter.*
5. *Grate a light layer of Cheddar cheese over the top – the more mature the better.*

TINNED SARDINES ON TOAST WITH KETCHUP

When I was off school sick, Mum would always let me get into her double bed, then go and make me a hot Vimto while I watched *This Morning* with Judy and Richard. It was like being on holiday, spread out in her queen-size bed. I would huddle under the covers, hoping that my temperature didn't go down too quickly. By lunchtime I would be painfully bored. Mum would be downstairs working in the office and would offer up Campbell's Cream of Tomato Soup with toast for lunch on a telly tray that had a cushion attached by Velcro, so it was just right for avoiding spillages on the duvet. Usually that hit the spot, but then I'd see Mum's lunch. It was sardines on toast with a slather of ketchup along with a minestrone Cup a Soup. I probably only wanted a taste the first time because it meant not going back to bed, but, surprisingly, I loved it. The tinned fish mixed with the butter, the sweet tang of ketchup and a swift grind of black pepper was the perfect alchemy.

2 slices of dense brown bread
Butter
1 tin of sardines
Tomato ketchup
Salt and pepper
Optional – a minestrone Cup a Soup

1. *Toast the brown bread.*
2. *Drain the tin of sardines.*
3. *Butter the toast.*
4. *Mush the sardines on top of the toast.*
5. *Dance ketchup over the top, then season to taste.*

ANCHOVETTE SPREAD ON TOAST

Our family friend, Jill Reichman gave my mum a pot of Peck's Anchovette fish paste after one Pesach meal. It's a South African anchovy paste, full of colouring and salt, and, heartbreakingly, it isn't sold in the UK. Mum has been known to pay for the extra baggage weight of friends if they mention a trip to South Africa, on the assurance that they will return with vats of the stuff (that is if they get past customs).

Bread or matzo crackers
Butter
Peck's Anchovette Fish Paste – find someone who is going to
    South Africa and get yourself a pot.

1. *Toast the bread (or prepare the crackers) and spread with*
    butter. Then slather a spoonful of the anchovette spread
    on either the buttered toast or matzo crackers. Trust me.

Eating In

There is a reason we created the *Table Manners* podcast. We wanted to talk to people, to understand them. I also wanted to combine food with occasion. Everyone knows that the quickest – and most pleasurable – way to really get to know someone is to sit round a table, in the informal space of a home, in front of a plate of home-cooked food, and eat with them. It's a perfect icebreaker when meeting a stranger. Food can also stir up any kind of conversation. It is an opportunity never to be missed.

The greatest lessons I've learnt have come over a home-cooked meal. Lessons in table manners, perhaps. But mostly lessons in life.

Eat for Forgiveness

It was a fish that nearly broke Sarah and me. University was awkward for me and in the third year I cut my hair into a bob and started to go to the gym obsessively, desperate to change my appearance. I wanted to shock myself into change, a new start. After two hours on a treadmill one evening, I walked into the front room to find it full of our friends and Sarah's twin, Samantha, professionally lounging in front of *Lost* with cheap wine and crisp packets strewn on the floor. Sarah and I were on a frosty episode that week, as was becoming standard, so through gritted teeth I offered a 'hello', then went to our dirty kitchen to fix dinner. There I found empty packets of trout and discarded trout skins left on filthy plates on the countertop for the flies to feast on. Fuming, I marched into the living room – interrupting their telly watching stupor – shouting, rather Shakespeareanly, 'YOU OFFEND ME WITH TROUT!'

Samantha and Sarah, with their identically confused faces, couldn't even muster a response. But my rage hadn't come from nowhere. Trout had become Sarah's fish of choice for entertaining, and could usually be found fermenting at the back of the fridge, in various stages of decomposition. When she cooked it, the smell was pungent and rudely lingered when left in a brimming bin within a humming, ventless kitchen. So yes, it was quite offensive. And yes, I was offended.

My fervently over-seasoned and zested tagines tasted awful, but at least they left behind the deceiving smell of spices and warmth. I longed for Sarah to return to making bacon sandwiches, or her mum's Turkish tomato and spinach rice. I wished she'd stop doing marathon television series sessions with groups of ten people. I also wished we were currently on better terms so I could have made a lighter joke about the whiff of her putrid dinner-party remains. I was so terrified of Sarah when she was disappointed in or upset by me, I think 'Trout-gate' was my masked way of attempting to fight back. But it wasn't my finest battle. I went to my room on an empty stomach, feeling like I had been slapped in the face by a fish, my head filled with the *Lost* theme tune and disappointment. If I could do it again, I'd have skipped the treadmill and been there for the trout.

Eat for New Friends

First day at my new secondary school, Alleyn's. I was wearing an oversized school uniform from John Lewis – to make sure it would last the year – and black Kickers, with hair down to my shoulders and a puffy face. It was the kind of face an eleven-year-old has when they're just about to grow into their future adult face but they're not there yet, so the nose looks out of place, the cheeks still retain the puppy fat and it's all just a bit . . . awkward. The classroom had a distinctive scent; zesty Impulse O2 or Vanilla Dreams colliding with Lynx Africa deodorant and the strong smell of onions.

Mr Friedlander, our elderly form tutor, called the register. A timid symphony of 'yes' and 'here' travelled like single-file dominoes around the classroom. Everyone on their best behaviour, eager to blend in for their first day. Then, from the back of the room, 'Ycs. Hcrc! Sir, it's actually pronounced Peneyaaatay, cos I'm half from the Canary Islands. It's a Spanish name, you see.' I took a look behind me to see a beaming face to match the cockney cheekiness of the voice. This was Jack Peñate. He looked older than the rest of the boys in the class and had an amazing confidence. I was impressed. Usually, it was the girls trying to be adult, and yet here was this boy, on the first day of a new school, already holding the class's attention, and so charmingly. I liked him and I wanted to be his friend. And that was before I found out that he had been on stage as one of Fagin's gang in Cameron Mackintosh's West End production of *Oliver!* the year before.

We quickly got into sharing information and soon discovered that both our mums were single parents, recently separated. We were desperate for our mums to be friends. Apparently his dad, Charlie Peñate, was the greengrocer who had introduced the iceberg lettuce (or was it the Canary tomato?) to the UK and he

47

had met Jack's mum Clare when they both worked in the Hard
Rock Café. Each story was more thrilling than the last, and I
would relay *all* this to my mum, every scrap of his narrative, as he
would my stories to his mum. By the end of September, Mum
and I had been invited to his house on a Saturday night for
dinner. It felt exciting, partly through pride in my new friend, but
also because I was being invited to dinner with my mum, which
made me feel incredibly mature: was this what the first month of
secondary school was meant to offer? I had always wanted to grow
up quickly – not to be recklessly drunk, smoke or have sex, but
because I longed to be in the company of adults, with food and
conversation at the centre. And now, within two weeks of turning
twelve, I was there.

Jack and Clare lived somewhere far, far away – Blackheath.
We took a taxi over the heath in the pitch black and pounding
rain, me nervous and excited about this evening of potential
matchmaking, my mum completely calm, but that was Mum,
ready to thrive in any social situation. Their house was filled
with Clare's parents' paintings, bookcases, earthy tones and
velvet furniture: cosy, erudite and chaotic. It was the opposite of
our house, but equally homely. We ate moussaka and chocolate
mousse in martini glasses at their kitchen table. Mum and I sat
next to each other like husband and wife, with Jack and Clare
on the other side. And Jack and I just watched our mothers
bonding over Marlboros and books (Mum had taken up smoking after Dad had left; I never really thought it suited her much
but was all for it in this moment). We would glance at each
other from time to time, communicating our silent agreement
that the night was going well. I think we were both so worried
about and protective of our mums, and in the same breath
immensely proud of them. We wanted to show them off and
light them up.

For us, it was the immediate comfort in finding a friend who could understand what the other was going through, making light of something heavy, that brought us together. Now I know that both Clare and Mum needed that companionship perhaps even more than their children. Our union was confirmed by Titus, Jack's older brother, nabbing a fag off Clare and jumping on the counter behind me and Mum to turn on the radio. He was dialling into his mate's jungle set on Kool FM. Next, he was calling up on the landline phone to get shout-outs for us all.

'This one goes out to a lady like Jessie,' said an MC through the crackly waves. I turned bright red and beamed.

'Make way for a lady like Lennie,' was next. We all burst into laughter.

Within two hours, two dishes, two bottles of wine and two shout-outs, Mum had invited them to Skopelos for the summer. Clare said to me recently, 'I remember thinking, this is completely bonkers, but I found myself saying, "Yes, why don't we!"' One of our most important, formative family relationships was built on a night of pirate radio, moussaka and chocolate mousse, but more beautifully, it was both families' impulsive embrace of each other, a leaning on a fuller future, together. Future Friday-night dinners, Sunday lunches, birthdays, summer holidays and Saturday afternoons at the cinema were spent in a gaggle. We loved being in the same room, eating from the same plate and living vicariously through Clare's wild stories of sixties Chelsea, the Rolling Stones, the Hard Rock Café, music, film, books and, of course, love. In a haze of full tummies, late nights, cigarettes, laughter, music and Cointreau, we grew and we learnt from each other. And over the years, we became a part of each other's history. The allure and charm of the Peñates and the Wares together never fades; it simply tastes sweeter and sweeter over time.

Eat for Indulgence

Everyone trusts me with the takeaway order. Because I order the lot. So no one will miss out. And although Sam will chastise me for the amount of plastic Tupperware that comes through the door, it will be forgotten about after a bite of the peshwari and a mop with a roti, because every dish and side dish and condiment was invited to our evening of eating in.

Eat for a Sense of Occasion

The Saturday-night curry we would get from Marks & Spencer, Deansgate, Manchester, on the weekends when we would visit my grandma (aka Gaga) will always remain my most nostalgic and cherished takeaway. Gaga loved an afternoon at the big M&S in town, going for a *shmy* ('a look around' in Yiddish) before heading straight to the food hall for salt and vinegar crisps, hummus and the whole ready-made Indian selection. Getting M&S food in the nineties was the equivalent of going out to a posh restaurant like The Ivy; it felt special and it was expensive. So that was our night in with our grandma, eating a chicken korma and lamb rogan josh in front of the telly watching *Catchphrase*, *Blind Date* and then *Casualty*, falling asleep from the feast and her overheated flat.

Eat to Be Fed

Sean was my Irish-Italian housemate in the second year of university, along with his American-Indian-Italian side-kick, Simon Sylvester Chaudhuri. They were clowns, they were adorable and they were the greatest cooks. But we feasted the best when our parents came to visit. When Simon's late father, Dr

Utsab Chaudhuri, flew over from Kansas, he would cook an Indian feast, filling the basement kitchen with the smells of lamb curry, coconut cashew rice and palak paneer, with a pakora in one hand and an arm around my shoulder demanding we all call him 'Uts' while he called us 'Buddy' because he could never remember anyone's name. Sean's parents would fix up an effortless pasta dish or a quick mushroom risotto. The pasta was always more al dente than we ever made at home, and their quick pomodoro sauce – made with the same ingredients I would attempt it with – packed such a flavour, which I am still incapable of recreating. Sean has found his way to London after fourteen years at sea, sailing around the world, living on Caribbean punch and relaxed time. The first thing he said when we sat down to eat at my house was, 'I just remember when your mum would visit, for two hours I would be lifting foiled containers and heavy cling-filmed pots of meatballs, chicken soup, roasted chicken and lasagne and bringing in the shopping she had got for you. God, she used to cook for us all, that woman.' She did. But then Uts brought warm, freshly homemade chapattis backstage to my Brooklyn Steel show.

Eat for Love

I've always imposed myself on Felix White. Year Five, he was the new boy in our class and I picked him out to be my boyfriend. He had no say in the matter; his wide blue eyes and sticking-out teeth would not win this fight. When he hid in the corner of the classroom if I attempted to hold his hand, or when he ran away from me in the playground, I realised his submission was somewhat unwilling.

When it was clear that being his child bride wouldn't stick, I decided he would be my *best* boy friend. He, Billy Hunt, Toby

McColl and I would hang out when I wasn't with Nancy, Christina and Zoe and we would go paintballing or for after-school teas together. I'd avidly watch them play cricket or join in with a game of football. I loved being with the boys; we could be goofy, grunt and still understand each other, or I could take on an increasingly commanding motherly role for my impressionable male friends.

We never went to Felix's house all that much. His mum, Lana, had been living with MS ever since I had known Felix. I remember her walking Fe and his two younger brothers to school for drop-offs and pick-ups with a walking stick and a warm smile. Only a few years later, the walking stick had turned into a wheelchair and by the time Felix and I were teenagers, Lana was pretty much bed-bound.

We spent Felix's seventeenth birthday at his house, eating pizza, listening to Oasis and drinking Strongbow, his mum in her bedroom next door to the kitchen. Felix pulled me away from the crowd so I could pop in to say hi to her. She was in bed, now unable to speak but still smiling. 'Doesn't she look beautiful, Jess?' Felix said as he stroked her hair so proudly. She did.

We were all aware that Felix's mum would pass away too soon, and as a group we took it upon ourselves to look after him. I foisted myself on him with too many phone calls and too many probing questions asking him to tell me how he was feeling, which in turn pushed him away for a few months. I was desperate to be his true confidante, while Amber and Alice gently backed off. We all loved him and we all cared about him eating enough, so I would use invitations over to my house as a ploy to allow my mum to obsess over his sustenance.

On 6 February 2002, a friend texted me in the evening to say Lana had passed away. Felix had been in school with us that day, flying high off memories from the night before when he and some of the other boys had gone to Milton Keynes to watch Oasis. He was 17, she was 46. The moment they had all tried to prepare themselves for had happened on an unassuming winter's afternoon. My knee-jerk reaction was to call his mobile. He sobbed on the phone. I was unable to stop myself crying, unable to say the right thing, but I was there to listen at the end of the line. The only thing I could think was how I wanted to hold him, to look after him, for all of his friends to be around him.

We all took the next day off school, congregating at my house to support Felix. There must have been about fifteen of us, all ready to surround him. We were lined up at the door as he arrived and each carefully hugged him one at a time, as if we were already at the funeral, propelled into a strangely formal and alien way to greet our friend. What I remember from that day is us sitting around the conservatory table. This table had hosted my friends for family meals, special occasions and endless conversations, but never like this. We sat there for hours and hours, surrounded by Pizza Hut boxes, listening to each other: laughing, crying and trying to ease Felix's pain ever so slightly. Felix was still in shock, but he told me that around that table was the first time he fully processed that his mum was no longer there. We sat around eating and talking, while Jack, Fe and Joel set about the regular task of seeing who could eat the most pizza slices (the most Jack has ever done is eighteen from Pizza Hut). Then we watched *Almost Famous* in the living room. Felix and I are still the best of friends, I still impose myself on him regularly, he still wears the silver wedding band Amber, Alice and I bought him for his eighteenth, I still buy him a cake for his birthday, even when I'm not going to see him that day. And I still think about Lana, who would be so proud of the man he has become and, hopefully, thankful that I never intend to let him out of my sight, ever.

Eat for a Sense of Humour

LA. The place of chance encounters, exhaustive schmooze and blind optimism, where the palm trees are the ladder to transcendental happiness. I have spent a bit of time there working with Benny Blanco on my second and third records, I've toured there and my sister Hannah lives there. With these stays, I have had my fair share of odd nights in LA. Many have begun at the Old Hollywood institution of Chateau Marmont with a glass of Whispering Angel (for my sins) and a touch of voyeurism, before ending somewhere far less glamorous. There's a strip club on Sunset that had a sort of inevitability to it. And there's a sense of culinary adventure there that can have you avoiding uni one night, and sitting at a supper club in an east-side bungalow the next looking down at a plate that is somewhere between a blood bath and a toddler's painting. The host might call it 'art on a plate', but the host also says they're 'all about tea'. And some stories are so surreal you still can't believe they happened.

Never was this so true than when I attended a dinner party at our friends' place. We were staying with Mark and Nat in Beverly Hills while I promoted my third record, *Glasshouse*, and they'd organised a dinner party. There were film agents there, the owner of a hugely successful medicinal cannabis company, a blockbuster action-film star, a high-profile personal trainer and the guest of honour, a health and life guru. Everyone – particularly Sam and Mark – was thrilled to be meeting this man. The world was intrigued by him and it was a real coup that Mark and Nat had lured him over, all in the hope of an informal education on his approach to life. Mark and Nat are the most perfect hosts: they are generous, thoughtful and have this knack of pulling together a group of strangers that will get on and create nights to remember. This evening held promise. We stood outside by the pool meeting each other, drinking wine, chatting and waiting to welcome the anticipated guest. He arrived late with his daughter, who was, almost inevitably, also his PR person. He was wearing shorts and flip-flops. It was perfect, rock 'n' roll; he was an anti-hero of LA schmooze.

We sat down to eat and found on each dinner plate a generous goodie bag of medicinal cannabis. I was sat in between the guru and his daughter, who told me they weren't in town for long and had a tight schedule of TV events and radio shows. And yet he took a liking to both the wine and the polite and extremely professional waitress. I couldn't stop studying him. He was fascinating and compelling, even after a bottle of wine, but I can't have been alone in wondering, 'What is he going to impart to us?' We waited with bated breath, taking in all the guru had to offer us, hoping for a cure for cancer, mental wellbeing, eternal health.

I looked through the bag of edibles, vape pens, mints and chocolate in between the mains and dessert, knowing full well I wouldn't be able to stomach them. The weed man must have seen my furrowed brow and confused face as he gave me a friendly holler across the table:

'Oh, try the yellow vape pen – light buzz, really lovely and mellow.'

When in Rome . . . I had a long chug on it. I am greedy and impatient, so when I wasn't instantly sure it had worked, I quickly inhaled another drag. Strawberry-vanilla-flavoured mist tickled the back of my throat.

As I sat back in my increasingly hazed state, I watched the scene unfold; the messianic man holding court with his followers. I got the feeling he was in his element. We had only seen this man through the eyes of his worshipers and the awestruck media coverage. That's the funny thing about chance encounters with fame: they either choose to live up to the expectation people have of them or they simply don't give a shit.

'Now, now, Dad, why don't we do a breathing exercise with this group of lovely people,' his daughter smiled.

'Yes, yes, *please*,' Sam and the film star encouraged.

'Ahhhhh . . . okay.' He projected with a fruity rasp, 'Are you ready?' accompanied by a dramatic clench of the fist.

'Yes,' the group replied exuberantly.

We sat in silent expectation, waiting for the secret to everlasting life. He told us to breathe in and out deeply thirty times and then to hold our breath for as long as possible. Apparently, it would make us feel amazing. I was unconvinced.

'Close your eyes,' he ordered. We closed our eyes.

'ONE . . . TWO . . . THREEE . . . YESSSS. YOU ARE GODS, LOOK AT YOU!' In and out we breathed, with a sense of purpose that reminded me of labour. He was encouraging us with the passion and presence of a sergeant major before battle. And we were his loyal troops, everyone trying their best to fulfil his method, slowly breathing in and out.

By breath fifteen I had opened one eye to see everyone deeply embedded in this transcendental practice – the concentration on Sam's face was like nothing I had ever seen on him before. Then came the moment to hold our breath. I managed about forty seconds before opening my eyes and bursting into an almighty fit of laughter. The vape pen combined with the heavy breathing had made the 'light buzz' turn into the almightiest giggles I had ever experienced. The kind where you try to squash it, but it bubbles back up even louder. This suddenly all seemed completely ridiculous. Everyone was a different shade of scarlet and their faces were stiff frowns, pursed lips and closed eyes, while the circus master jubilantly carried on bellowing, 'KEEEEP GOING . . . COME ONNN!' – the group fully at his mercy.

One by one they dropped like flies, Sam, the personal trainer and the film star hanging on the longest. I suddenly felt transported to the school playground. I never knew who held the record as I had to leave the table, knowing full well my laughter was disrespectful to our wonderful hosts and the master.

As I lay in bed, head spinning, regretting not finishing my main or staying for pudding, I vowed never to have an ice bath and a Californian vape pen at the same time.

Eat for Family

I open the door to Clare and Jack, their Sunday best on. It's 1999, so Jack is wearing Hugo Boss Man perfume, Patrick Cox loafers and a Paul Smith top all borrowed from Titus. Clare has her statement bright red lip on, a powdered face and smells of Chanel No.5, with flowers and a bottle of wine in hand.

'Hiya,' I say breathlessly, done in.

'Hi, darling . . . is everything all right?' Clare looks worried, already sensing a tension.

'Yes, I've just pissed Mum off, it's fine, come in!!'

In the background you can hear pots clanging, the oven door opening and Mum shouting, '. . . why do I bloody bother making a nice meal if the one thing I ask you to do is put the Yorkshires in at half past and you can't get off your arse to stop watching bloody MTV Base!! I'm absolutely sick of it!'

The monologue continues. 'This is not a hotel, Jessica! I am not your servant! Your room is a tip, my hair is *still* in curlers, my back hurts and now Clare and Jack are here. Hi, darling,' Mum finally looks at our guests over a pot of steaming cabbage.

'Lunch is going to be ruined because Jessie didn't get the Yorkshires in when I'd asked, so now the meat is going to be tough as old boots and everything will be cold. But don't worry, Jessie now knows the whole routine to "Love Don't Cost a Thing". Alex! Come and sort this bloody table out, will you, darling? Your sister can't be left in charge of that, it will look like we are eating school dinners!'

Alex, eleven, breezes in, kissing Jack and Clare, reconfigures the green table mats, plumps up the paper napkins and spruces the layout, giving it a certain *je ne sais quois* that I had failed to offer. Hannah is nowhere to be seen but will soon bounce down in a fabulous outfit and with a huge smile for Jack and Clare, miraculously coupled with a simultaneous scowl for her family.

Jack and Clare are unsure whether to stay in the kitchen and watch this passionate performance by my mother or to go into the living room where the fire's on and there are nuts and crisps laid out on the coffee table. They've seen this episode before. It happens every time they come over. In fact, it happens every time we have anyone over.

Eat Your Words

Felix and I were chosen by our school to take part in a nineties kids' show called *Eat Your Words*. It was an ITV Saturday programme on at the crack of dawn before the regular morning of television for kids would start. *Eat Your Words* was 'a game show for anyone with an appetite for words', according to a twizzle-haired Konnie Huq cutting her teeth on kids' telly. The late Mark Speight was the wacky chef in whites, but by chance, he wasn't on the show the week we were on. We had Sadie, dressed in a cute black-and-white waitress outfit, frilly pinny and a short skirt like a *Fawlty Towers* character. The good old nineties, where sexism was in abundance, and you could force feed children on television, as this show did.

On set, four contestants sat behind a larger-than-life-size roly-poly pudding, cream bun, cupcake and a pink mille-feuille, all with gigantic buzzers on top. An audience of enthusiastic sugared-up kids raised their hands on cue and whooped to the show theme tune. It was essentially a school lesson, on camera, in a room full of strangers, magnifying the absolute terror of answering a question with the promise of both ridicule and punishment; if you got a question wrong, you had to do a forfeit, that forfeit being to eat something disgusting. You might have to pick out prunes in flour with your hands behind your back, suck on lemons, or eat cold beans and bananas (or, in Felix's case, cold custard and carrots).

Our host, Simon, introduced us all, and asked us a few things about ourselves. I said I wanted to be Ryan Giggs, the girl next to me said she wanted to be a travel agent and Felix said he liked reggae music. I will always wonder how much reggae influenced his band, The Maccabees. Then the questions.

'How do you pronounce c-h-a-m-o-i-s?'

'What is the word for if you do something good in life, or pass an exam?'

I didn't thrive out there in the limelight. I forgot about the buzzer, I kept raising my hand to answer a question and I got the fifth letter of the alphabet wrong. But honestly, the food wasn't that bad, because truly disgusting food would have been child cruelty, or perhaps they'd just underestimated my threshold. My forfeit was a sandwich with something 'disgusting' in it.

'Ooooooooo, how gross is that? Is it sooooo horrible?' Simon asked.

'Nah,' I said, shrugging my shoulders and going in for another bite, 'it's pretty good actually.'

I had popped the entire premise of the show and it was time to be booted off.

We travelled back in the rain through Wandsworth Town with a commiserative tin of Roses and a stocking full of new toys and games. I felt like an absolute winner.

Eating Out

Apparently, life happens when you're making other plans. I'd like to respectfully disagree. Life happens when you're in a restaurant.

* * *

I was at the end of a long US tour, the final stop being a performance of 'Running' on Conan O'Brien's late-night talk show. But you don't perform late at night, so I was finished at 4 p.m., with a US promo face full of make-up and hairspray. I wanted to celebrate six weeks of being on a tour, sleeping in a bunk bed and drinking too much. I wanted to celebrate by drinking too much again that evening.

An old work colleague was in town and staying at the Chateau Marmont. Every day paparazzi wait at the entrance gate to snap celebrities staying or eating there. The only people I knew that actually stayed at the Chateau were superstars like Lana Del Rey, Florence and Sam Smith, or my producer friend Emile, who managed to convince a record label to pay for him to make a whole concept record there. He happily stayed in his suite for months. Parties at the hotel were exclusive and infamous, especially out at the back by the poolside villas. I only once got to the poolside, because I was out with Sam Smith for the night and he was meeting Rihanna back there for a drink. I've always only been an eager plus one.

On this particular evening, I found myself walking up to the hotel to meet a friend for a drink in the restaurant. Years before, we had worked together at a television production company and sat opposite each other in the office, offering to go and buy each other a coffee from Pret or a soup and sandwich from EAT. We got on well, she was interesting and warm and we both suffered under the same exacting boss. One Christmas break, Erika came back to the office completely in love. She had fallen for Edward Cullen, a vampire born in 1901 and the hero of the *Twilight* trilogy, a cultural phenomenon that had passed me by. It consumed Erika, and she spent the rest of the year passing her fan fiction over the desk for me to have a read. It was racy, sexy. This married mother of two had been awoken by a vampire and discovered a new lease of life. We both left the production company and separately set out to pursue our passions: to write and sing. Four years later, we found ourselves messaging each other via Twitter, arranging a catch-up drink at the Chateau, her home for the next year while they turned her book into a film. She was no longer known as Erika, of course, she was now called E.L. James.

I told the front desk I was there to meet Ms James, and the concierge muttered, 'Come this way,' leading me to a table at the back of the restaurant where a glossy-haired, smiling woman sat, so at ease in this rather daunting hotel. The concierge's tone completely changed when he approached her, becoming generous and charming, offering 'dear Erika' her usual, clutching her hand.

After a hug and a delighted shrug of the shoulders at how we had both got from a Holborn office to a Hollywood institution, I asked, 'Erika, what is your usual?'

'Ah, a bottle of Whispering Angel, sweetheart, the best!' she replied with delight.

I hadn't heard of it yet, but by the summer of 2019 it would be on every table. It was delicious and delightful and it seemed like angels danced in each glass. We talked and toasted our newfound careers, gossiped about the film that was in production and smoked in the corner like naughty schoolgirls. Erika was the life and soul of the room, a phenomenon; I watched in awe. After a couple of bottles, we said goodbye and I congratulated her on her success, thanking her for a glamorous evening of Hollywood surrealism. I should have left it there, but I ended up in a rave under the freeway with a new mate I had made in the smoking corner, the details of which won't grace this book. The next day I flew home with one of the worst hangovers of my life, whispering angels now obnoxious devils stomping through my head.

* * *

It was 1994 and Dad was taking me out for a Saturday. My parents had been separated only recently, so the usual outing with him was a late-afternoon trip to a Clapham Common café for a pot of tea and scrambled eggs on toast followed by a walk home across the Common. The café was called Teatime, a cosy traditional tearoom overlooking the Common that sat on the curve of the road just before you got to the Tube station. Although Teatime was on a ground and basement floor, it felt small, crowded, warm and inviting. Dad would have Assam and I would copy him; we would sit in the café waiting for the toaster, looking at the carefully baked cakes, and watch the heat of warm bodies and Saturday-afternoon conversations fog up the glass windows. I would closely examine my dad as he savagely spread the hard butter on his cold toast. The toast was cold because he was more interested in stealing whatever was on my plate than tending to his own meal. I have inherited both his attitude to caking toast with butter and his greed. Dad was always on a different clock to everyone else: scrambled eggs came at 3.30 p.m., his dinner was usually past my bedtime and I would know he was home because of the smell of fried garlicky vegetables in vats of olive oil. The smell would travel up to our beds before I would hear the faint sound of the *News at Ten* coming on.

One day Dad took me somewhere different, to the Streatham ODEON. This was quite unexpected, given that the last film he had seen at the cinema was *Top Gun* and that was only because he was obsessed with planes. He was trying to make an effort, I knew that. So we went to see *Dumb and Dumber* together, the most crude, awkward film to watch with your father, who was bound to find none of it funny. Luckily, he fell asleep. Afterwards, we crossed over the road to go to Wimpy. I ordered the cheese-burger on a wholemeal bun and the banana milkshake. He let me have it all. Sitting in that empty restaurant, with its stark fluorescent lighting, plastic tables and chairs, and the faint sound of Capital FM in the background, eating the most delicious burger, fries that sat in red gingham paper and drinking a thick, sugary milkshake that couldn't make it up through the straw, should have felt like a novel treat for me with my dad. But deep down there was an incredible sadness – for me, for him and for this odd and alien scenario we both found ourselves in. He was trying his best to fit into a part of my world that my mother had created so effortlessly, and I loved him for it, but this part of my world felt stranger and more bittersweet with him being in it. There's a time on a Saturday afternoon, especially in the rain or cold, when I will always think about my father, craving that cosy moment in the tearoom together, the warmth and togetherness, sad that it has not been relived more.

* * *

Tootsies had opened on Abbeville Road and I wanted a job there. This was at the beginning of the noughties when there was the influx of gourmet American burger spots opening up. I longed to be a waitress when I was younger, to pretend I was working at *Neighbours*' Lassiters or the Diner in Summer Bay, and now there was the chance to get a Saturday job right on my doorstep. Perfect. I passed the interview with flying colours, charming the manager with my significant interest in people, beef patties and French fries.

Tootsies was *the* place to eat – if you were hungover, if you were with your family and young children, if you were on a date. Before we even opened the doors on a Saturday morning there were queues for the fry-ups, and by the end of the day my feet were sore from a twelve-hour shift. Of course, I also ate my body weight in onion rings and order mistakes passed on by the grumpy cooks. I enjoyed it: I loved tapping the orders into the computer, I loved suggesting a fried egg on your burger or a side of chilli for your fries. I mainly liked talking to the customers – perhaps for a little too long – I was that trusty charming waitress you loved. And I *was* loved. I felt it. And never more so than when *Big Brother*'s second winner, the charismatic Brian Dowling, would come in and give me a hefty tip. He was hilarious, bold, on a meteoric rise to stardom, and I was at his table telling him that he wouldn't regret his order of the Jalapeño Burger.

I was a star. Or so I thought. After a few months of working there, the manager pulled me aside before a shift and told me, 'You just don't have the restaurant vibe,' and I was encouraged to look for another job. I went on to the perfumery counter at Peter

Jones on the King's Road. And I happily licked my wounds in their excellent staff canteen.

* * *

Following a week of painful silence in the house, I was the one to cave and text Sarah to ask her out for a reconciliation dinner. This had become a regular occurrence with me and Sarah – we would disagree, fall out, talk about this being 'the last time' we had to deal with this level of high drama and torture, ignore each other, talk to every mutual friend to try to absolve ourselves of guilt, and then have to meet in a neutral spot to 'have it out'. It usually ended in tears and, finally, a restored friendship. I opted for something fancier than usual, perhaps to give some edge to the fact that I was the one instigating it, even though Sarah had *clearly* been the one out of order. She had started the food fight.

So there I was at Vauxhall's Brunswick House on a Friday evening in 2011, waiting with bated breath for an emotional showdown, quietly delighted that there would be a good dinner amid all the drama. Brunswick House is a Georgian mansion on the Vauxhall roundabout. The restaurant is owned by a friend of mine, the chef Jackson Boxer. I had made my first ever solo music video there, 'Running', thanks to Jackson letting us borrow it one Sunday evening when they were closed for service. The house is filled with heirlooms, antiques and old paintings delightfully cluttering the walls, all for sale and all creating an incredibly romantic place to sit for a drink at the bar or for dinner amid the grandeur of hanging globes and chandeliers that light up the house. Sarah arrived and we offered a tenuously polite but stern 'hi' to each other. Was this the end of our relationship? Was she going to say she was moving out, or was I about to crumble at the carefully crafted words of a school debating champion? But before we could dive into who was wrong and who was right, I spotted the girl that Sam had been seeing in Brighton when we were broken up for two years. Although Sam and I had been back together for over a year by now, I had thought about this girl nearly every day since seeing a Facebook photo of them kissing in a Mexican doorway. I had painfully scoured through pictures of them on holiday – her topless and make-up free, cracking plenty of jokes, and him laughing in a way I felt he had never laughed with me. It had been a gut-wrenching discovery while on tour singing back-up for Jack in America, and I had obsessed over her ever since.

'Hold on, Sarah. It's bloody Dunya!' My heart was racing. I had played out this moment so many times and now it was happening in the middle of an intense conflict resolution.

Straight away, Sarah returned to being my devoted partner – everything about the trifle face slap was forgotten and we gasped together.

'She's seen you, she's hiding behind the bread bin,' my trusty sidekick said. God, I loved it that Sarah was there. She had heard me whingeing so many times, and had always listened, offering her take on each of the Mexico photos.

Dunya tentatively approached us with a paper and pen. Oh God, she was about to take our order.

'I'm ordering Prosecco,' I snapped before she got to us, thinking this would be a *huge* statement to my nemesis about my flourishing music career.

'Yes, you absolutely should,' said Sarah, always there to hold my hand.

'Hello, Dunya,' I said, like a prosecuting officer with the upper hand in the case.

'Hello, Jessie,' she said sweetly, with a cautious smile.

'We finally meet.' (The Royal Shakespeare Company came out at this point in the conversation and I was going full Helen

Mirren as Lady Macbeth.) She took a breath and smiled, wrote down our order and, for a second, I was victorious. Someone else brought our order over. Afterwards, I thought about how awkward it must have been for her. She hadn't done anything wrong, nothing at all. I wasn't with Sam when she met him and we both knew how great he was. I had forgotten my sense of sorority; it was not my finest moment.

Nothing got sorted out that evening between Sarah and me, because it didn't need to. We gossiped and laughed while I played her my new song, 'Wildest Moments', on my iPod. We drank a couple more celebratory bottles and we ate everything in sight. From what I remember – in between repeated sips of boisterous fizz – we devoured three sourdough bread baskets, which helped to mop up the delicious cuttlefish stew and aioli and a cod's roe dip. There was certainly a goat's curd in there somewhere and if Jackson's bavette tartare with cured egg yolk was on the menu, that would have been ordered. After a cheese board finale, we were eventually – and politely – asked to leave, as we had outstayed our welcome and all the other guests had gone home over an hour ago. Looking back, I'm more mortified about this than having had a fight with a trifle on a main road.

We didn't go back to Brunswick House together. But we've spent the decades going to restaurants and sensibly never overstaying our welcome. Nowadays the silences are generous and forgiving, as they always should be between friends.

Eating Out at Nando's

B lur or Oasis? E17 or Take That? The Beatles or the Rolling
Stones? Pizza Express or Nando's? Although I will always
appreciate the revelation of a Fiorentina pizza with extra pepper-
oni (thanks, Jack), for me, Nando's is my winner and I have
remained loyal to peri peri chicken. As a teen it was the afforda-
ble other to Pizza Express. It was lively, friendly, quick and tasty
and was within walking distance of Sam's family house. What I
love about Nando's is that every time you set foot in any establish-
ment, you know what you're getting and you will leave satisfied.
It never lets you down (even if you may let yourself down while
eating there).

The secret to Nando's is to keep it simple. With a guest, always
order the full chicken platter and get four regular sides. Then
share one bottomless Coke. You can have a little flexibility on
which sides, but not much. It's simple. Yet somehow in the
course of my love affair with Nando's, things haven't always run
as smoothly as choosing what to eat. The venue for the easiest
decisions has somehow become a place of misrepresentation,

miscommunication and miserably recovering from fashion mistakes.

* * *

I like to think I have good table manners. I like to think that I am polite to waitresses and waiters. So I feel that I need to apologise to a waiter called Jack, from Nando's Brixton.

We were there before a show, the usual place to meet before going to Brixton Academy over the road. Sam and I were going to see The Pogues for their annual Christmas show. The Brixton Nando's isn't the fastest Nando's on a normal day, but on a gig day it is usually a bit of a shit-show. There's always a bouncer outside taking and calling out names and telling people, 'It's gonna be a bit of a wait, mate. Show day.' However, there is also always a bustling energy and anticipation in the air, next to the smell of flaming chicken and the thundering sound of the ice machine.

It used to be our regular spot: for going out with friends in Brixton, taking my little brother out to the Balham restaurant or an easy date on Streatham High Road. And now it is usually saved for show days at the Academy. I always loved the ritual of ordering the whole chicken platter, deciding the sides, perhaps branching out with the premium sweet potato mash instead of fries, stealthily sharing the refillable Coke between four of us. Our order is the same every time: Sam always wants the peri peri fries and coleslaw and I want the posh peas, rice and a corn on the cob, but I will also trade a couple of spoonfuls of rice for a taste of the coleslaw and a grab of the chips. There's a reassuring sense of occasion when you go to Nando's, especially when that is tied in with going to a Brixton Academy show. That evening, I ordered our exhaustive list of differing heats and sides, took our wooden flag and went to find a seat. There we waited, sipped on our one Coke and waited some more. Finally, a sweet, fair-haired young man with a name badge that said 'Jack' approached us with most of the order, placed it on the table and pleasantly mumbled, 'Enjoy.'

'Um, hi, so sorry but I think you've forgotten the peri peri chips,' I said politely.

'Nope, think this is all your order,' he replied.

'No, I definitely ordered the peri peri chips, as I didn't fancy the rice today. Hold on, let me try and find my receipt.'

I flail around in my bag for the proof, throwing Carmex, Tampax, old chewing gums and hair slides onto the table. How is it that even though I was handed the receipt less than five minutes ago, I can't find it now? Why can you never find a train ticket when the conductor comes?

Eventually I fling out a crumpled-up piece of paper and shoot it to Jack. He takes a look and walks away, returning minutes later with the peri peri chips. It was a minor mistake by Jack, tiny. I could have just said 'thank you' as I took the plate of chips off him, but instead I chose to look him in the eye and turn into a character from 24. 'Don't fuck with me, Jack, I know my order,' I said. The words came out of nowhere and were really quite unnecessary. A heaving Brixton Nando's on gig night is not a fitting place to play out your recent binge through the last series of 24. Perhaps his name triggered me away from Stockwell Road and into the mind of Jack Bauer. These are all feeble excuses, but I still wonder why the words came out of my mouth and why, in that moment, I was so close to becoming my mother in a hangry state of mind.

Jack looked back and laughed nervously, confused and taken aback, as I ferociously dipped a chip in some garlic sauce. So I'm really sorry, Jack, I just lose my mind in Nando's.

* * *

We sat at our regular booth in Streatham Nando's one Saturday evening in 2003 to grab a quick bite. We were off to the ODEON to watch the early 7.30 p.m. screening of *The Matrix Reloaded*. No need for fake IDs anymore; we were adults now, young and in love.

As we waited for our full platter to come, we held hands over the table and smiled at each other.

'I really love you, Sam,' I said confidentially, looking straight into his eyes.

'Touché, babe,' he cooed back at me. I never corrected him; in that moment it was perfect.

* * *

I always wanted to wear knee-high boots. And in 2003 they were everywhere – back in fashion. Unfortunately, my legs wouldn't allow it. I could never zip them up to the top so always had to opt for a cowboy boot or a suede Primark slouched pair. So I'm still puzzled as to why I thought it was a good idea to suggest them as a gift from my boyfriend. But there we were, Sam and I, holding hands as we wandered through Covent Garden, ten months into our relationship, one eye on him and the other peeled for a potential boot I could gently draw his attention to. 'Oh. Those boots are cool,' I said to a pair of grey suede knee-highs with a swashbuckling black leather clasp sitting in the window of Shellys shoe store. It was casual but direct enough to nudge him in the right direction. We strolled on, stopping in Muji, Lush and Stüssy, and picking up a Starbucks gingerbread spiced latte before heading back on the Tube to South London.

I forgot about the boots. Then, the night before my family and I were flying to New York for a white Christmas, Sam and I exchanged our Christmas gifts. We were sitting in his bedroom, listening to music, talking about the diners we would visit and the Knicks basketball game we had tickets for once he got to New

York to join us on Boxing Day. I knew straight away what the long rectangular box was. Dread hit the pit of my stomach. He had got me the boots, and now I had them up close, there was no way that zip was going to make it to the top. There were ten minutes of trying, now down to my knickers and with bloody fingers from pulling so hard on the zip, but the boots couldn't make it past my calf. Crestfallen, I admitted defeat, mortified that my boyfriend had had to watch my legs lose this battle.

'Babe, it's not a big deal, I will buy you some Huaraches in Brooklyn when we are out there, or a new handbag. I can take these back,' Sam said with an arm over my shoulder, safe in the knowledge that trainers and bags will always fit.

'Let's go down to King's Road now and try the bigger size,' I panicked. 'I think if they were one size bigger, I could get them up. It's late-night shopping today – we can get them now and I can take them to New York,' I said in desperation.

'Sure, babe,' Sam replied, understanding and easy-going as ever.

We walked downstairs, me now back in my jeans and scarlet-faced, holding the shoe box. He called out to his mum that we were leaving.

'Did you love your boots?' Tessa, his mum, asked.

'Ah, they didn't fit right actually, unfortunately,' I said meekly.

'Oh, that's such a shame! Sam was so excited to give them to you, and they are so beautiful. I have to say, I love them . . . you know what, can I try them on? It seems silly to take them back when I can pay you for them, Sam.'

She placed one boot on her slim leg and in a whoosh, they were on her, just like Cinderella's missing slipper. Suddenly I didn't feel like schlepping to King's Road. Instead, we went to Streatham High Road's Nando's and shared a full chicken meal, one half medium, one half hot, with plenty of sides.

Alcohol, in All its Forms

Year Six and Zoe Burrows had invited us all over for a sleepover on the condition that we promised to sneak our parents' alcohol into our bags. Having only dabbled with Kiddush wine at Passover in a tiny thimble and the occasional sniff of wine or whisky on my dad's breath during bedtime stories, it was with some trepidation that I approached my mum's alcohol cabinet. Never the boldest of the group, I settled on one tall can of cupboard booze and hoped for the best, not sure I even wanted to get drunk yet. The six of us ran up to Zoe B's bedroom, our weighty backpacks banging against our backs with every step. On a secret operation, we tipped our bags out onto the bed, eyeing up our stolen prizes, whispering about the best route of action to reach a state of 'drunk-drunk'. I don't think any of us actually wanted to get drunk, and the discussion was short-lived, as Zoe B's mum overheard us in cahoots, intervened, gave us a stern lesson in alcohol abuse and called our parents. I was mortified when my mum collected me the next morning. In the car, with my head hanging low, I whispered, 'Sorry.' My mum told me never to steal alcohol from her again, and after a short pause she added, 'Especially a can of Newcastle Brown Ale, which I only use in stews.' And then she laughed.

* * *

It was the summer of 1998, and everyone was still talking about the Coen brothers' film *The Big Lebowski*. We were all obsessed with Jeff Bridges' character 'The Dude', and with that his customary drink of choice, a White Russian. We were in Skopelos for our annual summer holiday, Clare and Jack in tow along with Family Sweeney. It was the first year I was allowed out at night and I was ready to show my older sister that I deserved my place. After dinner, we negotiated some drachmas off our parents and drifted off into the night, in agreement that we wouldn't see them until the next morning. My mum wasn't worried about our safety, given the size of Skopelos and the fact that everyone knew each other. We sat in International Café, waiting for the island's one nightclub to open, Hannah rolling her eyes as I threw myself into entertaining the group. During that first round of drinks I was a smash hit, allowing each White Russian to last a good couple of hours. I can't remember any Greek batting an eyelid serving up stiff drinks to a thirteen-year-old, then again, I might not have done, but I was delighted by my mature restraint.

From the International Café to Captain Morgan's for a pre-discotheque midnight drink. The music was louder, the party was on the tip of being in full swing, and I now wanted to keep up with my older sister, her best friend Rachel, and Chris and Emma Sweeney. When Chris egged me on to have another White Russian, I said, 'Give it to me!' I couldn't resist; I had to stay in the race. And this cocktail tasted like dessert.

A free shot of sambuca here, the odd shot of tequila there, we shouted 'YAMAS!' over the sound of Mousse T's 'Horny' and before long we were marching towards the nightclub. We reached

Kounos, the broom cupboard-sized club in town, after six hours of drinking and I knocked back the free Heineken on arrival. I was feeling on top of the world.

'I. AM. THE. DUDE!'

The group found me pacing the balcony of the club performing a solo dance piece for the locals with the help of Fatboy Slim's 'The Rockafeller Skank'. By the time DJ Shadow's 'Organ Donor (Extended Overhaul)' kicked in, it was 6 a.m., it was time to go home and it was inevitable that I would throw up. The night ended with me trying to stomach a croissant from the bakery, the team cackling at my misfortune and me subsequently vomiting it all up into a palm-tree urn by the swimming pool at our hotel.

The next morning my mum woke me and my hangover up, throwing open the black-out wooden shutters in the apartment.

'WE CAN NEVER COME BACK HERE AGAIN! YOU HAVE SHAMED THIS FAMILY, JESSICA!' My head throbbed. I skulked to the pool at 2 p.m., hid in the shade and clutched my Coca-Cola bottle, waiting for the next wave of nausea. It was the first and last time I entertained a White Russian.

WHITE RUSSIAN

60ml vodka (90ml if in Greece)
1.5 tbsp Kahlúa
1 tbsp cream

1. *Fill up a short tumbler with ice. Pour in the vodka, Kahlúa and finally the cream.*
2. *Enjoy it – just don't have four of them.*

* * *

Everyone would order a Goldschläger and lemonade for their second drink of the night at Potent Soundz. This was our regular burst of drum and bass – sometimes on a school night – at a bar on Wandsworth Road, where we were allowed to dance and drink, even if not all of us had the right fake ID. Aside from studying for A levels, our mates Ben and John would diligently host this night and be on the phone, booking anyone from Adam F to Friction. Who needed the dark maze of Fabric, prayers that your fake student card would work and long waits for the first train home from Farringdon? On nights I didn't want to drink, I could drive to Potent Soundz, park the Cinquecento on Queenstown Road and drive home in fifteen minutes, stinking of cigarettes. My ears would feel like they were bleeding from standing too close to the speaker when Sam, aka 'DJ Once', was warming up the crowd or 'supporting the headliner', as we'd say with relish.

Was it true that Goldschläger had real flakes of gold in it? Did the gold flakes cut the lining of your stomach, making you get drunker more quickly? Reading up, the amount each bottle held of gold amounted to around 50p, but that didn't stop you feeling like a luxurious, cinnamon-liquor-drinking lightweight. It makes me shudder to be reminded of the taste of it, because inevitably that taste is associated with the nights I didn't bring the Cinquecento out. On those nights, I'd be throwing up in the bar's toilets or on the 37 night bus home, missing DJ Zinc playing, cursing the day I was introduced to such a horrendous drink.

* * *

The success of Amarula at the 2006 San Francisco World Spirits Competition – where it won a gold medal – must have trickled down to us 2007 Sussex Freshers. Or it must have been on offer at the ASDA Brighton Hollingbury Superstore down the road from the campus, because we were all drinking it like we were

Henri de Toulouse-Lautrec or Pablo Picasso discovering absinthe for the first time. As well as Bulmers and blackcurrant cordial, bizarrely, it became *the* drink to accompany a night out. I tried to convince my family that this South African drink, with its notes of pear and guava, was better than Mum's cherished Baileys in front of Christmas telly. It absolutely wasn't and much like my 2007–9 Primark wardrobe of pirate slouch shoes, plaid shirts, gypsy skirts and low-slung leatherette woven belts, it was thrown out by the end of university.

* * *

When it comes to wine, I know what I like, but I don't know that much. I've tried wine tasting many times, yet still haven't trained my taste buds to understand what makes a particularly great grape. Never ones to waste, my friends and I usually get so drunk by the end of a tasting that the poor wine teacher is offering us extra bread and politely asking for 'a bit of order' as we drunkenly shout over each other in the boozy classroom. I once met a friend at Hackney's L'Entrepôt and asked for a glass of something 'that goes down like Ribena', much to the horror of the sommelier. I know nothing.

But I do know that I have some idea of wine tasting don'ts from watching a music producer who was sitting opposite me at Gjelina's restaurant in Venice, California, and using his girl-friend's mouth as a spittoon. After tasting the wine, he slowly regurgitated it into her mouth. It was like observing a mother bird feeding their young. 'Mmmmm, yummy!' she said, gazing into his eyes. I always wondered if it went down like Ribena.

A Free Bar

When you work in music, or I suppose in any of a number of seemingly glamorous jobs, you get a lot of invitations to events – where there's a free bar that comes your way. If you go with someone you know who's invited too, you can throw back drinks in the corner and stalk out canapés. Often it's easier to go on your own, pray you know someone on the red carpet and make a quick exit. Some of the time, it's just so much easier to stay at home. Most of the time, though, its infinitely improved by inviting one of your actual friends. Most of the time, but not always.

When you're invited to a charity football match at Old Trafford in 2015 commemorating David Beckham and the class of '92, and you are a supporter of this charity, the club – and of course a life-long fan of David in every way – you invite your friend who is United through and through. This was Jamie, who Sam had spent the majority of his student life with in Brighton, going to drum-and-bass raves, worshipping the UK hip-hop scene, both working hard at Uni but harder in the pub. I loved being in

Jamie's company, so even though a weekend away in Manchester together was a first for us, I was confident it would be fun and that he wouldn't let me down.

Jamie and I got the first train up from Euston and dropped our bags with my mum's cousin Elizabeth and her husband Dennis in Whitefield, season ticket holders and the cause of my fandom. After a cup of tea and a serious debate on the dream line-up, we headed off to Old Trafford where we found ourselves in the director's box, a few seats down from the players' friends and family. We knocked back a few free Aperol Spritzes, shoved in some free sandwiches and scoured the room, feeling more than a little out of place.

I only knew the people from the charity who had invited me and my friend Akua, who worked at Adidas. But we clearly managed well enough and were invited to the after-party later. A triumph. But it started at 11 p.m. and we had hours to fill until then. Hours I inevitably decided would be filled with food. I'd met Rio Ferdinand in a Glastonbury dance tent the year before, and he'd said, 'If you're ever in Manchester, go to my restaurant.' So that's what we did, sitting down at Rio's Italian restaurant, Rosso, an hour later with Akua and her friend. We clinked our necessary prescription of Espresso Martinis, mindful of the need to stay alert for what was already destined to be the best party we would ever step foot in.

'OH. my. God. Jessie! Ronaldinho just walked past us and looked me directly in the eye,' a gleaming Jamie shouted over the house music. And we weren't even at the after-party yet. We had another drink, settling in to our life of glamour. Once we saw Ronaldinho slope out from across the room, we decide it was our cue to make our way after him. Our moment had arrived.

The party is at a basement club, protected by bouncers and top-secret passwords. As we descend downstairs we have a bird's-eye view of the intimate set of party guests. Paul Scholes, Nicky Butt, Edwin van der Sar and Mikaël Silvestre all look up. The whole team is here! And as I watch a teenage Brooklyn offering Baby Spice a bit of sushi from the buffet, I realise we have essentially been invited to a Beckham family do. Jamie and I bounce down the stairs like contestants on *Strictly*: wide smiles, bright eyes, but completely pissed. Jamie is so drunk by this point he offers to buy Jamie Carragher a drink at the free bar. Thankfully, Jack Whitehall and Serge from Kasabian are just as giddily drunk as us, knocking back shots with David Seaman. Or at least I *think* it was Seaman.

I soberly remember I have been invited by the charity, so hold off from any more drinks, focusing my attention on the moment I will finally get to meet David Beckham. I won't be telling him about the fact that his National Portrait Gallery postcard has been on my mother's mantelpiece for ten years. Or that only a few years ago I fell off a New York barstool when he walked into the hotel. Or that I had to leave said hotel because I was so flushed. No, I will be professional, a fellow ambassador to the charity organising this event, a peer, a sober ally in a sea of drunken merriment.

Jamie returns from the loo to tell me he chatted to Ryan Giggs over the urinals. I'm starting to worry that Jamie's moved beyond Dutch courage to be that annoying drunk mate you wish would get a cab home early.

'What do you mean, you chatted to him? What did you say?' My tone is verging on tense.

'I was pissing next to him – I think I pissed on his shoe, actually . . . well, I needed to say something, I am standing next to Giggsy with my cock out! So I said, "Hey, mate, do you know where Jessie Ware is?"'

'No, you didn't,' I say, mortified.

'Yer. And he said, "Who's Jessie Ware?"'

I'm starting to seriously question my choice of guest.

'Hey, listen, J,' I say. 'Why don't you get some of that sushi over there? Looks really nice. Could soak up some of the booze, babe.'

'Naaaaahhhhhhhhh,' he replies, double parked with a Haig Club whisky and another Aperol Spritz.

I decide to leave him with Akua and her friend, who seem entertained by him and better able to manage his level of inebriation. Instead, I seek out Louisa from the charity, David's right-hand woman for this event and the person who's invited me.

'Jessie, I need to introduce you to David. Have you met before?'

'Only in my dreams . . .' I reply under my breath.

'Huh? Can't hear you . . . Oh David, come here, I want to introduce you to someone who works with the charity. She's a singer and a huge United fan – this is Jessie Ware.'

Oh my God. This is happening. I don't think I am ready. And then I'm shaking David Beckham's hand.

I mumble something unimpressive and he replies politely and then that's it, my moment with him has passed. I walk away to locate my drunk friend.

But before finding him, I get stuck into a conversation with Emma Bunton. This night is getting progressively more surreal. Perhaps I could have tried to say something more memorable to David, or Emma, but I was feeling like a fish out of water and ready for bed.

Little did I know that Jamie had made sure the Beckhams wouldn't forget us in a hurry. When I went back to our table he was sitting, head in hands, recounting a scene I'd just missed.

'Well . . . I was licking my wounds after Giggsy wouldn't chat and I saw David and Victoria standing on their own just over there, so I thought the stars had aligned and it was my destiny to go over and tell him how much I love them.

'Well . . . I went and put my arms round the both of them but I kind of fell into them and before I could start speaking, Posh had told me to get my hands off her and their bodyguards had stepped in.'

The train ride home to London the following morning was a sombre affair. Between his regular trips to the bathroom, I reminded Jamie of his consumption and confidence throughout the night. He was mortified and painfully hungover, the most brutal reminder of how he had abused the bar. The lesson here is: never take your newly qualified teacher friend to a free bar if his icons are going to be there, unless you want to make sure you're both remembered.

I checked back with Jamie to corroborate this story. Apparently, he offered Peter Crouch a drink at the bar and asked Jamie Carragher for a dance. But of course.

* * *

When you're invited to bring five friends to a private dinner party hosted by new and exciting ex-Noma Mexican chef Santiago Lastra, you select carefully. I invited my mate Ben and his new girlfriend Jess, Sam (of course) and a pregnant Samantha. She was flying solo that evening so there was one more space at the table. 'Why don't you invite Zesh? He is always up for it,' Samantha suggested. I have known ZeShaan and his twin brother Soufian for over twenty years. Tooting boys, dancing pros, the life and soul of every party. We were always at Potent Soundz together, Fabric, a Maccabees gig, a friend's wedding. Within the space of an hour of meeting ZeShaan, he will have probably charmed you with his flirtation or with polished renditions of a particular brand of early-noughties garage. On another day, imagine Dizzee Rascal, rendered perfectly, word for word, line for line. We expect nothing less, supplicants to his bombardment of raps. He's a bit of a star, our Zesh.

The evening was set to be in the chef's temporary test kitchen, so we all schlepped to Acton on a cold Friday night to a terraced new build on a quiet suburban road. We didn't realise that his test kitchen was also a temporary home to him and his brother, Eduardo, flown over from Mexico to help develop the restaurant, which was set to open in 2020. As we walked through the kitchen and into the gazebo where a makeshift dining room had been set up, we passed huge steel machines and alien equipment that looked like it had come straight out of *Breaking Bad*. Santiago planned to turn foraged ingredients into nostalgic plates from his Mexican home, and it was an intimate affair, as though we'd come over for dinner as friends rather than for an organised feast. We were guests in their home; enthusiastic guinea pigs for Santiago to try out his food experiments on.

ZeShaan and Samantha had already arrived and were given drinks by the sommelier. Zesh had managed to knock back a fair few glasses of natural wine, and was leaning on the kitchen counter like he was hosting the Mexican brothers, already calling the head chef 'Santi, Santi'. Samantha and I shot each other a look. We sat down for the starters: oyster carnitas with sea buckthorn and habanero in a warming umami broth; short rib – which Samantha broke her vegetarianism for – with a sweet potato mole and crème fraîche; horse mackerel with a peanut cream, fermented beets and horseradish. Plates of fresh corn tacos wrapped in leather envelopes, foraged ants that crunched in your mouth, bursting of citrus. All these courses were washed down by a Georgian orange wine, a Slovakian Cabernet Sauvignon or a Riesling called Little Bastard; it was a new way to be eating Mexican food in London. Before long, Zesh was throwing drinking water behind his shoulder to wash out his glass for the next wine pairing, then knocking back Ben and Jess's portion of the bottle.

'We may be outside in a marquee, but there is quite clearly carpet on the ground, ZeShaan, not grass. Heaven forbid you would actually drink the *water*!' Samantha barked under her breath, as sober as a judge despite the fact that I was bullying her to have 'just a sip, for the baby' at each pairing.

By the time Ben and Jess had arrived and played catch-up, we were onto the main, a whole chargrilled octopus that Santiago plated up with such precision, placing the charred tentacles as tenderly as a new mother puts down her baby. It was pride and joy among a crowd of increasingly pissed adults. We were making our own tacos, with a shared pair of scissors to cut the tentacles off the octopus one by one. ZeShaan had decided to rip his off – with quite a struggle – like a tough loaf of bread.

'Zesh, can you not touch the whole octopus, mate' – 'Use the bloody scissors,' Samantha and I tag-teamed.

ZeShaan had started to ignore us, while Sam told us both to chill out and stop making a big deal of him.

'Santi, Santi, my brother!' his arms were hanging around the chef's shoulders now. He was like that uncle at the wedding, the one who wants to have a deep and meaningful conversation about your love life, but who can't quite make it through the first sentence. We rolled our eyes. By the time the chocolate steamed tamale with corn-husk ice cream arrived, ZeShaan was no longer interested in eating. Instead, he was now proclaiming to be the Mayor of Nunhead and talking about showing the brothers the sights of Southeast London. We shoved him into a cab back home. Sam said Samantha and I had been too hard on him. Sam is usually right.

Santiago was finally able to open his restaurant KOL in October 2020. Sam and I were invited to the friends-and-family soft-launch lunch. After we had congratulated him and his brother on the opening, Eduardo tapped Sam on the shoulder and said, 'Hey, why didn't you bring your friend? Zesh was his name, right?'

I sharply butted in with, 'Oh no, no, no, *God* no! We are so sorry about his behaviour at your house before, he was just a little too drunk and merry, having too much of a good time.'

Eduardo replied: 'We loved him! He came to another pop-up of ours after that – he's such a great guy.'

I texted Samantha on the way home. We both agreed that we were in fact the sticks in the mud and that a free bar isn't worth a thing if no one's drinking it.

* * *

Alice Levine poured me a third glass of Lambrusco sparkling red. It was delicious and apparently natural. She was hooked on the stuff. The *My Dad Wrote a Porno* trio were over at my house, joining us for our podcast, and between mouthfuls of Mum's trifle we were fitting in sexual innuendos wherever possible. They were a hoot, and extremely generous with their offerings of natural wines – something I wasn't familiar with. There is a myth that natural wines don't give you a hangover. This has been offered up to us through the naked grape vine with such confidence. So that evening, we attacked those natural wines with a focused alacrity, celebrating an evening of laughter and a morning with a guaranteed fog-less head.

It is my privilege to share with you that this myth is entirely unfounded. The morning after the night before, I woke, as did the rest of our guests, with one of the worst hangovers I've ever experienced. This could have been heightened by the fact that I was unknowingly pregnant, but everyone else felt equally dreadful. So natural wines absolutely do give you hangovers – especially if you drink four bottles.

Chocolate

By the beginning of 2007, I felt all the performances and caricatures I had been enacting at university for two years come to a painful halt. Sam was now at Brighton University studying photography and I started to question every move he made or thing he said. I was jealous, fretful. I felt like I had reached the third year fraudulently and wondered why I had wasted so much energy on entertaining people with a diluted, ditsy version of myself. A version of myself I now seemed stuck with.

I thought university was meant to be a decisive and empowering age of independence, but I found myself tearfully on the end of the phone to my mum five times a day – if Sam wouldn't pick up, that is – needing constant reassurance. Sarah was always there to listen, but I knew I was bleeding her dry. I was confused and irrational and the more I needed the people I loved, the more unpleasant I became.

Finally, I started seeing a therapist weekly in Shoreham. I would get the bus there and talk about everything from Sam to my newfound OCD that involved frantically cleaning the kitchen (albeit badly), to my father leaving. I was always regarded as 'the strong one' in our family, so I was surprised that my father leaving came up so much, after being buried deep, deep down inside of me. I remember my therapist crying one week when I spoke about the discovery of my father having a new child. I was shocked, assuming counsellors were meant to say little and stoically help you navigate your way to some sort of conclusion. We cried together, just for a second, and in that moment the impact of my sadness meant that I didn't need to shrug it off. Being with my therapist was the hour of the week that I anticipated; I would leave her box room exhausted but ever so gently healed. After every session, I would visit Lidl – right by the bus stop – for a box of Leibniz chocolate biscuits, the fake Guylian chocolate shells my mum used to give me, Florentines – anything to guide my fuzzy head and heart back into the real world. In that comforting taste of sweetness, I took stock of the past hour and years.

Fish

My grandma, Cecilia Keell (Gaga, we called her, Pat to everyone else) lived in a small flat in Cheetham Hill, Manchester, opposite a yeshiva. She was on the top floor and there was no lift. If she wasn't picking us up from Manchester Piccadilly Station, we would hop in a cab and make our way under the grey blanket of Northern sky to her flat, past the Boddingtons Brewery tower, up the high street, past Kwik Save, past San Rocco's Italian and into Park Lea Court. As we pulled up outside her flat, we would hear a warm 'HIIIYA' hollered out of the top-floor window and see a wrinkled arm offering a hasty queen wave. If the aroma had not seeped out of the open window, you would be engulfed by the sweet smell of fried fish as soon as you opened the door to walk the three flights of stairs.

Gefilte fish or plaice dunked in matzo meal and fried was my grandma's version of a cup of tea. And even though you would also have a boiling hot cup of Manchester tea in a thin china mug laid upon a cotton laced doily, it was the fish that welcomed you. As I have grown older, I now understand the value of a thin china cup: it keeps the heat just that much longer.

'Giss us kisses,' Gaga would say as she approached you unsteadily, with a scrunched-up smile and two arms up ready to clasp your face for a smooch. I loved going there, seeing her – the most vivacious woman I have ever known – cuddling into her M&S pastel jumper and the scent of Oil of Olay on her skin. We lived a long train ride away (she passed away before Virgin made the fast train from London to Manchester) and didn't get up to see her enough, but whenever I was with her, she brought comfort and clarity to my naïve eyes.

She was brought up in Birmingham as Cecilia Newton, one of nine children, and was made to leave school at sixteen to support and feed her siblings. Her mother had died when she was young and I remember her telling us how her father had been extremely hard on her. Even though she had a beautiful name, when she was working at a toothpaste factory the manager decided to call her 'Pat' as it was simpler to say, and it stuck. Pat Newton, who might have been related to Isaac Newton her mental arithmetic was so good, and who wasn't Jewish. She converted to Orthodox when she met my grandfather, Morley Keell, and spent a year living with his Russian mother, Minna, learning how to be a good Jewish woman and wife. My mum said that her parents fought like cat and dog, but what kept them together was an intense physical attraction; they fancied each other like crazy.

Gaga's gefilte fish – or 'chopped 'n' fried' as she called it – was famous in Manchester, and I was reminded of this by a friend and teacher of mine, Aviva, just the other day. Aviva is teaching me for my bat mitzvah, something I decided to do this year. I am older than my grandma was when she learnt to speak and read Hebrew, but somehow it keeps taking me back to this remarkable woman, brought up within a totally different faith but still with such a tenacity to learn, adapt and wholly embrace a new culture and religion, all for love. Gaga used to babysit Aviva, who once lived round the corner, and as she says, 'My Grandma Betty and your Grandma Pat used to sit and have a good gossip at the table while I listened in.' Aviva remembers Gaga bringing over her chopped 'n' fried fish balls and preferring them to the sludgy, sad-looking boiled ones her grandma would make. Gaga and Betty would play bridge together with another couple, Nat and Ina Goldstein. Pat, Nat, Ina and Betty, all sitting around, deep into an afternoon game of bridge, with my grandma joining Nat in drinking a small tumbler of whisky while the other two women had a more reserved cup of tea.

Nothing surprised Gaga, not even her eldest daughter Maxine eloping, aged nineteen, and having a baby, then divorcing quickly after, or her son Erroll going off to live in the Bahamas, marrying Miss Bahamas, then moving to an ashram in Kerala and becoming a Buddhist. I think when both Maxine and Errol passed away before her, she started to question whether there was a God.

She started to have mini strokes – known as TIAs – when she was about ninety-one and the doctor told her that she had to stop driving and drinking full-fat milk. She laughed at him and said semi-skimmed tasted of wee and that she wasn't going to stop at ninety. She believed that Greek yoghurt was the cure for everything: on your private parts for thrush, on your sunburnt skin instead of aloe vera. And a spoonful of honey was nearly as medicinal as the thumb of whisky she would have in front of *Countdown* every evening. The drink would be accompanied with a small bowl of salt and vinegar crisps. When we introduced hummus to her in the late nineties, it was just the ticket.

She would sprinkle a little sugar on her salad with a lamb chop – it was the only way you could get a salad down her. The contents of her fridge could have fed you for two weeks. The options: beef sausages, Vienna sausages, Bloom's salami (all kosher), an omelette, chicken soup, lamb chops. She would make sure she had smoked salmon and cream cheese from Manchester's famous and beloved kosher deli Titanics, with fresh Manchester bagels (the chewiest and best) or fresh challah buns. And before you had finished your breakfast on the last day of your visit, she would be planning which sandwich you'd be having for your train journey home. She was a feeder – a giver of love, enthusiasm and wisdom. She would always slip you 'just a little something' at the end of the weekend, a fiver or tenner that she would pull out from the corset she had hidden in her bedroom wall. It's where she kept all her money.

My mum still has Gaga's thin china tea cups. And they still make the best brew.

GAGA'S CHOPPED 'N' FRIED

500g fish (a mixture of cod, hake and plaice)
1 white onion, chopped
1 egg, beaten
Pinch of sugar
3 tbsp matzo meal
Salt and pepper
Sunflower oil

1. *Use a mincer if you have one or a food processor to mince the fish. Add all the rest of the ingredients (apart from the oil) to the minced fish and mix well.*
2. *Cover the mixture and put it in the fridge for an hour to marinate.*

3. *Divide the mixture into even-sized balls. Heat lots of sunflower oil in a frying pan.*

4. *Wear a shower cap (if you don't want to smell of fried fish for the rest of the day) and when the oil is hot put a few balls into the pan at a time and cook for a few minutes until brown, turning them over to make sure the whole ball is the same colour.*

5. *Once cooked, lay the balls onto kitchen towel to soak up the excess oil. Serve with chrain.*

* * *

I never thought Streatham High Road would be the epicentre of my romance with Sam Burrows.

It started at the Horse & Groom on a balmy end-of-summer night in August 2002, among a gang of friends seeing off our mate Tom, who was heading to Japan after a long love affair with Muji, Covent Garden. Everyone was hanging on to those last summer nights and I was hanging on to Sam's every word. They were, in truth, few and far between, but when he did say something I was enthralled. Everything he said was considered, respectful, quiet and then, once in a while, he would laugh. He smiled before he laughed, but that laugh took over his whole body, all six foot two of his gangly frame, turning him into Frank Bruno. I was drinking a J2O, dressed in a turquoise off-the-shoulder H&M number, bootleg jeans from Gap and pointy satin bright red flat slippers that made me look like a therapist from Hampstead. But I had a glorious tan and huge Claire's Accessories hoops, which helped with my Jennifer Lopez illusion. We all went back to Sam and his brother Joe's house on Wavertree Road after the pub and headed to the attic, where Joe turned on N.O.R.E.'s 'Nothin'' and the boys smoked weed. Lots of it.

I was in heaven, surrounded by boys who weren't from Alleyn's, who were able to keep up some kind of conversation even after smoking the fattest spliffs I had ever seen, who lived and breathed hip-hop and graffiti and were utterly charming to me. They were cool and they were different to my other friends – it was exciting. Both my girlfriends Alice and Amber were having serious relationships (and sex) and seemed a little less available than before, and the boys from school were enjoying Café Cairo on Landor Road where they could smoke hash, or the Goose & Granite on Clapham Common for cheap pints. I was ready for a change and this set of friends was it. Sam and I got each other's number as he led me to the door when I left at 3 a.m., both pretending it was to 'reminisce about Honeywell', our primary school. I had butterflies.

We tried, unsuccessfully, to meet up for over six months. I would spot him on Christchurch Road in his mum's Peugeot Estate learning to drive with her as I sped home from school, which would lead to a text like *'think I jus saw u wiv ur mum?!'* He would offer a polite, friendly text back, but he wasn't exactly making a move.

Perhaps I ignored Sam's attempt to woo me at my sacred eighteenth birthday party in October of that year. He had heard I was having a party and texted asking to come. I pictured him arriving with five unknown mates, underdressed and not knowing what to do with him. I said something like *'Sorry 2 many ppl, Mum will kill me!'* The night was a marquee in the garden with bowls of chilli, beer and boxed wine from Calais, Titus DJing and me kissing Fe by the bins. But I wouldn't let that missed opportunity pass.

Saturday, 9 February 2003
Jessie Ware: Hey Sam, hope ur gd. What r u up 2 2nite?
 Fancy a drink? (1.03 p.m.)

Sam B: Heyy sorry 4 l8 reply. workin. sounds gd. where?
(4.08 p.m.)
Jessie Ware: I'm in Streatham @ my mates so cud meet u
after work (4.20 p.m.)
Sam B: gtg home first but ur a diamond. K. Baroque on
high road @ 9.30? (4.37 p.m.)

Although a bit miffed at such a late start for a date, I said yes and got ready with Amber for five hours. Baroque was a newly done-up cocktail bar on Streatham High Road that was next door to the beautiful Art Deco ABC Cinema, lost to a Fitness First and, later, luxury flats. I had been at Amber's all day, hoping that Sam would be available.

The night before had seen me sobbing down the phone to Alice and Jack after witnessing Matt Weeks getting familiar with a beautiful girl from another school at a house party. I realised that I was always going to be just his friend and I was tired of trying to read between the lines; it was a one-sided, unrequited love. I needed to get over it. And what better way to do so than to text the two boys I didn't mind using my phone credit on? Sam and Nathanial. Nathaniel was a confident older guy from Brixton who Jack had been in the National Youth Theatre with, who wore Converse, smelt amazing and who I had danced with at Jack's eighteenth. He made me nervous, in an exciting way, and he said yes to a date, too, on the Sunday. Just like the 137 bus, two boys had filled up my weekend with two different dates.

To meet Sam, I wore my trusty Gap jeans and the R. Soles heeled camel cowboy boots I had got on my eighteenth birthday from the King's Road. I had a black vest on underneath a show-stopping see-through black Miss Selfridge crochet top with a tie in the middle and I wore an overpowering amount of Jean Paul Gaultier perfume, borrowed from Amber. Nervous and light-headed, I got the 255 bus to the bar. Sam had on black Iceberg jeans, a Diesel black hoodie and black Air Max 90s with a patent black tick. We ordered cocktails and sat on a slouchy sofa and all of a sudden we realised this was a date. We talked about both our mums being social workers, him being born in a bathtub in Brixton and growing up in a feminist cooperative, while I tried to impress him with my love for Billie Holiday and Aretha Franklin. We were so different, but somehow met in the middle. The conversation was easy and by three raspberry Mojitos in, I was playing with the string of his hoodie and asking him why we had met up so late.

'I work on the fish and meat counter at Sainsbury's and I didn't want to meet you straight after work as I was worried my hands would smell of fish.' His hands were rough from bathing them in lemon juice and scrubbing them so hard. My heart melted.

The night ended with him putting me into a minicab, giving me a kiss on the cheek and sending a text saying he hoped I got home okay. I crept into my mum's bedroom when I got back and whispered, 'I'm home. I was out with Sam Burrows – do you remember him from primary school? His mum's a social worker.'

'Oh lovely, darling, yes, his mum Tessa is a very good social worker. And gorgeous.'

'Oh and, Mum, he works on the fish counter at Sainsbury's,' unable to stop filing off information to her.

'Oh good, darling, swordfish skewers!' she said drowsily and fell back to sleep.

So as not to be rude, I dutifully went on the date the next day with Nathaniel. He talked about himself throughout while I thought about Sam, then, when he was about to drive me home, he kissed me. Then he asked if I was a virgin. 'I'm not about to straddle you in the car, for God's sake! Just take me home, please,'

I demanded, my outrage perhaps giving away that I certainly was a virgin.

There was a film my mum had shown me called *Crossing Delancey*, an eighties film set in New York about a woman who doesn't know whether to marry a humble pickle vendor who dips his hands in vanilla extract ('It kills the pickle smell,' he says) or an arrogant married man. She chooses the pickle vendor. His name is Sam.

TABLE MANNERS

Things I have learnt:

1. Don't leave a used tissue on your plate – Sandi Toksvig will judge you.
2. Start your hot food before everyone has been given their plate at the table, otherwise you are just going to have lukewarm food. Kiefer Sutherland says so. And to me, that makes a lot of sense.
3. Be polite to waiters (sorry, again, Jack from Nando's!).
4. When being invited over for dinner at my mother's house, don't say that you are missing an election debate between Jeremy Corbyn and Boris Johnson as you walk through the door, after my mum has slaved away in the kitchen for five hours to make you a Christmas meal. Your episode on *Table Manners* will never come out.
5. Don't also then talk about animals being killed when Mum has made you a vegetarian meal – it really ruins the Chrimbo vibe.
6. Don't then tell Mum to shut up when she is trying to lighten the mood of the painful hour with you by singing an Earth, Wind & Fire classic. It's just incredibly rude.

7. Never have a scented candle on while you're cooking or at the table when you eat, but do bring one over as a thank-you present, it always goes down well (thanks, Nigella).

8. Don't be offended by trout at a dinner party.

9. Do as your mum says, especially in the kitchen.

10. Be one step ahead of your mum, before she begins a tirade about your laziness.

11. Ordering in is fine, and sometimes necessary if you have cocked up a recipe (as George Ezra can attest).

12. Say 'darling' more often. Be more Lennie.

13. Don't try to blow torch your rum and raisin crème brûlée, you may set your hand and house on fire.

14. Don't listen to your mum when she says, 'You're doing it all wrong!' and certainly don't give her the blow torch – she will actually set her hand on fire.

15. Trifle will go down well with everyone – certainly Grace Dent, who won't be able to sit down she is enjoying it so much – but don't expect it to be the showstopper at a wedding.

16. Don't spit wine into your new girlfriend's mouth in front of someone who idolises you. Save it for behind closed doors.

17. Leave the skin on the onions when you make chicken soup; it will bring out the colour.

18. Learn to make matzo balls. And then teach me how to do it.

19. A diced onion in rice with water, a lick of oil and a chicken stock cube, put in the microwave, will solve stodgy rice and you will never go back to the pan.

20. Make a 'b' and a 'd' with your hands to know which side your bread and your drink goes on if you're feeling a little Julia Roberts in *Pretty Woman*.

21. Whispering Angel will give a shocking hangover, as will natural wine.

22. Pet Nat makes you sound incredibly fancy, but it's a little like drinking fizzy grapefruit juice. And there's nothing wrong with that.

23. It's okay to live for champagne.

24. Don't discuss what your mother could have done better with the dish when it's been served. It will piss her off and be uncomfortable for your guests. You will be the one who looks like a dick.

25. When you are invited on the podcast, and you have requested a Sunday roast, please don't then arrive forty-five minutes late when we have cooked a roast to perfection. It will make us look like shit cooks when the chicken comes out dry.

26. Please don't decline our food – albeit politely – when you've already given us an extensive dietary requirements list. We are not in LA now, Dorothy.

27. Don't then go and order an egg-white omelette on Deliveroo. It won't travel well and there will be some judgment on our behalf.

28. Don't then tuck into the banana bread for afters when you said you were gluten intolerant.

29. Always over cater. Always over share.

30. Do let friends be drunk. Don't be a stick in the mud.

31. Don't ever sacrifice Baileys over Amarula. Always say yes to a dinner party. You never know what could happen, who you will meet and what you will eat.

Aeroplane Food

It was 2013 and my band and I were in transit at Stockholm's Arlanda Airport. It's slightly chicer than most airports; they have interior design shops and an excellent food hall full of Swedish gourmet sandwiches, cured fish, cod's roe – the lot.

With my open gravlax salmon sandwich on rye bread with cream cheese in one hand, I turned on my data on my phone with the other. I was waiting for something to come through to my inbox that was worth switching on my international data for.

Ding. *Email from Daniel Tuffin: Subject: FWD – Prince Remix of Wildest Moments*. It was there, clear as day, looking right at me. This was no longer a dream. I stood in the middle of the causeway of the busy Swedish airport and hollered at my bandmates in Starbucks, 'It's here! It's here. Come, come, come!!!!!'

A very funny thing had happened to me a few months before, and I thank the Internet for this. Prince had started to mix my song 'Wildest Moments' into his online DJ sets. People had tweeted me about it. I didn't believe it, but there, with my own eyes, I saw him playing my song about Sarah. That would have been enough for me, but then his management had reached out to ask if he could remix it.

My bandmates and I huddled round each other, knowing our flight was boarding in ten minutes, and waited for the download to finish. We listened out of my tinny iPhone 4 speakers and the sound we heard didn't provide a lick of a Prince guitar – no, it was the sound of panpipes. We listened through.

'Hmmm,' Joe, my guitarist, said.

'Right,' I added.

'Ahhh . . . this harks back to his nineties era with the pipes,' Alex Bonfanti – my bass player and extreme Prince enthusiast – said.

'It's not what I expected,' I whispered, feeling blasphemous even questioning the greatest artist of all time's work and the panpipes that were taking me back to the Peruvian hills. The remix didn't come out, but it was the highest accolade for Prince to have considered my work. I have lost this remix, I'm ashamed to say; it was like it vanished into thin air. No one heard it apart from me, Prince and my band, but I feel lucky to even have the possibility of uttering my own Prince story, which took me from Arlanda Airport to Paisley Park, if only for a few moments.

* * *

I wouldn't recommend giving it the big one on a morning easyJet to Barcelona for your best mate's hen do, especially when you are the maid of honour and have organised for fifteen girls to go to the Primavera festival. What happens is, you drink too much on the flight and then have to take yourself to bed early because you're no good at daytime drinking at altitude and apparently can't stay up later than 10 p.m., even when you have nothing to do but put penis straws in your best friend's drink and dance at a festival.

* * *

Joe Newman is my guitarist. He's been with me from day one and provides constant entertainment, astute Spotify playlists, feminist Marxist wisdom and cringeworthy moments, especially when it comes to food. He's sensible – bordering on frugal – with his money and the way he eats, so if there is the option of a free meal, he grabs it by the horns.

He will stuff the show-rider offerings into his pockets before we leave a dressing room and will always politely ask if 'anyone wants this last glass of red?' when, really, he's desperate for the last drop. When he's not on tour, he survives off vats of low-cost homemade dal, and always returns to me looking much slimmer than when we finished a tour.

I love my conversations with Joe through departure lounges and in the passport queue. He's fascinating and thoughtful, and he's the bank of so many memories – my ride or die. But on planes – planes where you still get a free drink and a meal – Joe turns into a horrendous, albeit courteous, vulture. If I pass him on my way to the loo, I am guaranteed to see him with two empty mini bottles of Cab Sav and extra pretzels. And that is on a modest, restrained day.

Not that I wish to use it, but here is Joe's imparted wisdom on how to get the most free wine and food on a plane, because there *is* a system:

1. Wait until the meal service has finished – keep your eyes peeled for who declines a hot meal.
2. Change your order from chicken to the vegetarian option in an attempt to fool the staff into providing a second meal.
3. Alternatively, make friends with the air stewards in the galley.
4. Pocket the leftovers of your friends' cheese wedges, bread rolls, butters, as you never know when you will be getting your next free meal.

5. Eat the second meal and savour it; it could be your last.
6. Eat the third meal, if the staff member has clocked on to your tricks and returned with two hot meals to call your bluff.
7. Ignore the embarrassment and disgust felt by your neighbouring relative or bandmate.
8. On arrival, accept the fourth – and final – hot meal that is waiting for you by the aircraft doors in the hands of said steward as you step out to leave the plane.
9. Feel no shame. Never stop blagging meals.

* * *

There is nothing quite like the initial sip of that first G&T on a flight with your family to your summer holiday destination. The soothing taste of accomplishment, the cold gulp of relief. It is to be quietly cherished, while a just-about-to-nod-off baby lies over the two of you, spread-eagled, tethered by the compulsory infant belt. The baby could be knocked out from waking up at the crack of dawn, or because of the 80-per-cent-alcohol anti-bacterial wipe you just pulled out of their mouth, or it could be because of that perfect cabin white noise before take-off. You don't question it; perhaps now he will sleep through the whole flight?

You look over to your daughter, who is watching *Minions* on the iPad, headphones on, content and excited for the holiday. She is oblivious to the fact that her tray has become an open gin bar *avec* salt and vinegar Pringles boxes, crunched Mediterranean-flavoured tonics and miniature Tanqueray bottles.

It's a small trade-off for the pile of Pringles in her lap, which so complement her Fruit Shoot aperitif.

You cheers with your husband, sink into your chair, take a quick sip of your disappearing drink and give each other a peck behind your reapplied face masks. It is summer 2020. There is another family to the left of you: a milk-bottle lid rests on a can of beer; there's a half-pecked apple with toddler teeth marks in it and a negotiation going on.

'I want TOAST,' says the little boy.

'They don't have toast, for the tenth time,' his mother percussively whispers before the dad shoves a chocolate button in the boy's mouth.

The second G&T, well, it's less delightful; the ice has melted, and while you pre-empted this ten minutes ago, the stewardess is avoiding eye contact so she doesn't have to offer you an extra glass of cubes. Still, you drink it, a little woozy from lack of sleep and the altitude (God bless the altitude adding that extra oomph). You question soaking it up with the emergency pain au chocolat you got from Pret for the kids, but if you move to retrieve it, you will potentially wake the sleeping baby in your lap. Now your right leg is experiencing mild cramp. Thankfully, Chris Sweeney is at the back of the plane and has come to scope out the toilet queue at the front, so he assists with retrieving the croissant. You thank him with an emphatic eyebrow lift to compensate for the mask hiding your appreciative smile. Sod it, they never knew there was a croissant to begin with.

'I. Need. TOAST!!'

'There is no toast. End of discussion. Do you see a toaster on this plane??' Mum puts on another episode of PAW Patrol and throws another chocolate button at him, before his dad interjects. 'Say please, Daniel. Say pleeeease.' No judgment; we are all just trying to survive.

Croissant dandruff lies all over the baby's hair, hard to remove. You ever so slightly stretch your legs out, making sure the baby doesn't roll off, nearly slipping on the discarded banana skin lying in a sick bag on the floor. Your husband has drifted off. You eye up one more drink as the passive-aggressive stewardess marches through with the food cart. You could do with some pretzels or a soggy cheese-and-ham microwaved sandwich.

The words 'DID YOU KNOW ABOUT OUR 20 PER CENT OFF ALL DUTY-FREE DEAL WITH JET2 . . .' boom over the tannoy. The baby is awake now, startled by the noise, and he's a little upset. You go into action mode, covering his ears and leaning into him with a slow shushing sound. It is working, but Daniel's dad, who has backed a couple more beers and a vodka and orange, has started a loud maths lesson with Daniel in the form of chocolate-button addition. His face mask is now skew-whiff and settling under his nose, which irritates you. The baby manages to drift back off – as does your husband – and so now you're on your own, watching the Minions' guitar solo on mute and contemplating the Egyptian Magic cream in the duty-free magazine.

The third G&T is quenching and cold, but the condensation drops onto the sleeping boy's face. That could have woken him, but it is your over-reaching grab of the flight attendant asking for the 20 per cent off the eye cream that does it. That's it. The stationary aeroplane bar crawl is over, but it was fun – and fuzzy – while it lasted.

* * *

Two weeks have passed and certain developmental changes have happened to my son; he is now a lout and a flirt who hollers 'EEEEYE – YAAAA' to any person that gives him eye contact. It's entertaining, albeit a tone too loud for an evening flight. I spot Daniel's dad walking through the aisle (still with his mask under his nose) and see a good tan from his two weeks away. Our friends, the Bolton-Greens, sit in front of us with their daughter, Estelle, popping her head up over the seat to join in with my son's yells, giggling through the gap in her front teeth and enjoying a spot of peek-a-boo. We order a G&T each, but this time it's a bit of a disappointment. It doesn't even touch the sides, perhaps because we have drunk Greek wine and the 5 . . . 4 . . . 3 p.m. gin and tonic for a fortnight. There is no sigh of submission and relief, so we neck the first drink so as not to make the same mistake of letting the ice melt.

I eye a Pot Noodle on the paper menu that is stuck to the back of the seat, conscious that my four-year-old hasn't eaten anything apart from a reluctant mouthful of spaghetti bolognese for two weeks. It is an immediate success and I shoot Sam an 'I told you so' look while my daughter shouts, 'More, more, more, Mumma, I want *five* mouthfuls.' BINGO, we have a winner.

Estelle catches the enthusiasm – and a whiff of MSG – and launches herself over the top of her mum's seat to demand a fork full. They all fall madly in love with the chicken and mushroom pot of deliciousness, until it turns all too aggressive and the enthusiasm resembles a scene from *The Walking Dead*, me batting away tiny grabbing hands that dart through the gap between the chairs in front and round the sides, resisting the groans of hunger to my left and right by shoving speedy mouthfuls into each child's mouth. I can't get it into them quick enough and even when we order two more, I can't keep the arms at bay or stop Estelle from stealing a long noodle out of my son's mouth. I taste a pot to 'check the temperature'; it is even better than I remember it tasting as a ten-year-old: saltier, denser and moreish.

International Cuisine

I dream of food from other countries. I watch television shows set in Vietnamese food markets, spend hours on YouTube looking at how to make a Japanese soufflé omelette, read books about Italian cooking, move rapidly from tour bus to local restaurant. My honeymoon was militantly planned by food stops. We had three breakfasts, four lunches, snacks and dinner. We would walk for miles away from the hotel, in the freezing cold because I *had* to find the soft-serve soy ice cream with the doughnut in a Kyoto food market, or the sleepy jazz bar on the outskirts with the greatest Japanese whisky list I've ever seen. I've had my best sushi in a Tokyo office block, eaten hotdogs in a secret New York speakeasy hidden behind a telephone box, cracked open a bucket of fresh crabs' legs and corn by the Seattle waters, had beautifully soft slow-cooked lamb at a Devon farm, tasted my finest pili pili prawns in North Goa and hunted out the dirtiest Martini in Ubud. But in the spirit of honesty, Anthony Bourdain I am not. When I think of my biggest adventures, my deepest cultural immersions, I'm not sure I've triumphed in gastronomical excellence.

Forgive me. Don't judge me when you read what is to come. If I could do it again, I wouldn't have slept in a haze, I wouldn't stay in the same hotels, and I definitely wouldn't get on that boat. I would, however, go to all the restaurants, the stalls, the cafés, the markets – always to the food.

* * *

Sam and I went to Marrakesh when we were twenty-two for an anniversary. We stayed in a beautiful riad, a traditional Moroccan house set around a courtyard – palatial yet bizarrely within our student budget. All the rooms were themed, and we opted for the 'blue room', a tadelakt haven of brilliant turquoise and aquamarine with a huge tiled bath built into the wall. In the day we would go to the Yves Saint Laurent gardens and get lost in the souks, coming back with three of everything: bags, spices, tagine pots. We were never going to get past the easyJet hand-baggage officers.

By evening, I practised my GCSE French on the cab drivers: 'Ou est le blonde hashish, monsieur?' The first night of our trip found us out of town, waiting in the cab outside a dodgy-looking discotheque, anxiously waiting to pick up some hash. Incredibly romantic.

When we returned to our room I had one toke of the joint and pulled a whitey, once again embracing the romantic potential of the trip. Sam – a stoic and dedicated smoker – persevered. Unsure if he was hallucinating from Morocco's finest fumes – and with me passed out – he could hear a familiar song that had been exhausted on Radio 1 that year. Through the walls of the house, it played over and over again.

'If I lay here . . .'

The melody bounced off the stone walls, darting around the room accompanied by an echo of timid groans . . . politely pleasurable. Sam climbed over my lifeless body and looked out of the window onto the courtyard, wondering if he really had been smoking hash or something else entirely.

A glow from a corner window on the first floor of the courtyard directed Sam to the origin of the sounds. Sam was a reluctant voyeur to someone's love-making. He tried to wake me, I didn't stir, so he spent the rest of the night with his hands over his ears trying to block out soft whimpers and Snow Patrol.

The next morning, we sat down for breakfast next to a quiet couple from the UK. We realised that the hotel only had two rooms occupied.

He has never been able to listen to Snow Patrol again.

* * *

In the late spring of 2003, Alice, my old friend Clara and I had been 'travelling' for a couple of months in South America. I say 'travelling' because we weren't exactly roughing it – it was an extended holiday, with a planned itinerary. We were to be gone for three months, too long to be separated from my and Alice's long-term boyfriends Jack and Sam, and not long enough to say we fully dug into Central and South America. And we spent most of it looking for internet cafés so Alice and I could send a love letter home via Hotmail. Clara emailed her parents. She was thrilled.

Accepting every opportunity to eat local food has got me into trouble before, but strangely this never deters me from doing it. I will always search for the full food experience, sniffing it out wherever I go and obediently indulging. But that trip taught me a few things I am happy to impart:

– The 2 a.m. Ilha Grande Brazilian fried chicken out of a food truck will be a warning shot. You will be holed up in bed (and bathroom) for a day with only memories of the sound of Samba and too many Caipiroskas to sustain you.

That and visions of sucking on unrecognisable parts of the chicken.

– The fateful 2003 trip to a Peruvian McDonald's, just outside Lima's airport, will be a stern reminder that even our trusty friend Ronald McDonald cannot save you from being hospitalised. That funky-looking – neglected – gherkin condiment next to the ketchup and mustard does not need to be tried, my friend. Even if you have not seen it in any other McDonald's before, even if you can't be sure it's the cause for the missed flight, just hedge your bets and avoid.

– It is always worth eating the local food.

– The 'Comida Por Kilo' signs that are scattered over Rio will offer the most wholesome plate of food that will nourish you and restore the balance of the Caipirinhas on Ipanema Beach. The feijoada bean stew will be fresh and cheap and taste better than any of those slices of pizza you went for the night before. The low-key peri peri chicken place around the corner from your Ipanema hostel is addictive and, dare I say it, beats Nando's.

– The fresh fruit stalls with shelves of tropical fruits that you point at and they squeeze into your own unique and delicious juice soothe any hangover and revitalise you after late-night dancing on the steps in Lapa where you tried to recreate the Snoop and Pharrell 'Beautiful' music video.

– If the long, thin organic sausages at the small spot on a cobbled street in Cuzco where we went for a gourmet English breakfast count as 'local', eat them, too. They tasted better than the Llama we tried, I have to admit.

* * *

Our trip ended with a six-week stint in Mexico, and after gherkin-gate I was slightly more wary of the road-side options offered up during long coach trips across the country. We were heading straight to the east coast of Mexico where the water was calm and the beaches were idyllic. On these coach trips, I would opt for the tamales, the corn husk still hot from the griddle – a safer option of starchy maize with a lick of mole – or, if I was feeling slightly more adventurous, fiery rajas. The earthy smell of corn and banana leaf on hot coals would fill the coaches at every stop, such a distinctive scent of Mexico yet strangely reminiscent of home and of Mum's roast potatoes in the oven with their rooted, sweet tones.

By the time we reached Isla Mujeres, an island off Cancún, I had exchanged new food experiences for a daily cream cheese bagel bought from a kiosk run by an American girl. We were in paradise: white sands, aquamarine waters, with Daddy Yankee or Tracy Chapman humming out of every drink hole. Chastising the capitalist hedonism of Cancún, we would sip our happy-hour banana Daiquiri while swinging on a hammock and toasting our wild adventure. Then we would go back to the hostel kitchen to fix up a spaghetti bolognese. While we stirred our homemade sauce, Luc, a French-Canadian ex-Club Med lost-boy-cum-hostel-worker would saunter in and splash balsamic vinegar in the pot. He was cock-sure and had a soft spot for Clara, who hadn't had much luck finding a holiday romance yet because if we weren't talking about our boyfriends to each other, we were long-distance calling them, or talking to potential suitors about how much we wanted to call them. We were seriously blocking Clara's chances of an overseas dalliance.

One week into our stay on Isla Mujeres, Luc invited us tuna fishing and, tired of our bagel–beach–bolognese routine, we decided to go 'for the experience'. Or, to put it in simpler terms, we wanted to write something other than 'I miss you' in emails to our boyfriends. And it looked like Clara could be weakening to the French-Canadian's tenacious advances. The next day, we headed off to the dock to meet the other unsuspecting guests. The day unfolded not quite as planned.

10 a.m.

There were the two handsome tattooed Swedish blokes we had seen in the local bar who were due to fly back home the next day; the witchy hostel owner; an attractive Mexican lady with long dark wild hair; a couple of fun Americans called Amy and Ryan, clinging onto the last taste of spring break and two young Slovakian girls – nervy newcomers to the crew. A beautiful, plush white yacht was docked on the makeshift jetty and at the wheel was a portly middle-aged man with a bright white sea-captain hat. This was Captain Donald, or 'Don' as he liked to be called. He ushered us on board with an American accent, obviously delighted by the horde of young sailors coming out with him. 'Goooood morrnin', sailors! Come on board, beers are in the back, get comfortable!' he sang to us all.

Bob Marley was cranked up and we set sail, immediately heading to the top of the deck – the tan always a priority – with a cool *cerveza* in hand. Life was good, the sun was shining, we were on a yacht for the day with international strangers, careless and carefree, frivolous and easy-going. That was until forty-five minutes into the trip, when my stomach reminded me that I was terrible on rough waters. So down I went to vomit overboard, nibble on a cracker and stick to the Coca-Cola. I wondered how I would stomach the catch of the day later. Still, I had time to get accustomed to the sickly lull of the boat. Everyone was getting to know each other, talking, learning about what had led them to the 'Island of Women' and where their next destination would take them. Alice and Clara would chime together, holding court while I tried to get back to feeling a little more normal. Luc was below deck tying his hair into different styles, starting his day with a ketamine breakfast and suggesting we all got in the hot tub onboard.

2 p.m.

We had been in South and Central America for over two months, travelling through hot spots for the finest cocaine, but it had passed us by. Even when I used to go out raving, it was only ever extended into the wee hours by a can of Red Bull, never by taking pills. I promise. My school group had always got drunk and everyone smoked weed now and then, but in hindsight we really were incredibly innocent.

So by the time Luc had emerged from the yacht's en-suite with his fifth hairdo, unable to say anything remotely conversational, we were unimpressed. Having perked up a bit, I was preoccupied by our next meal, calculating how long it would take to catch the fish and then cook it. It was a calculation that suggested we were not eating for another good few hours. The boat anchored and everyone jumped into the sea, not a fishing rod in sight. It was so strange; no one was complaining about not eating. Of course, I later realised it was because everyone on the boat apart from us three and the two Slovakian girls were on a shitload of coke.

'It's 2 p.m., guys, when do you think we are going to eat?' I asked under my breath to the girls.

'I don't know. Have you got any of those crackers left?' Clara replied.

4.30 p.m.

Hours and hours passed (two hours, to be precise) and still no food. 'I'm really tired, thirsty and hungry and so I'm just going to ask Captain Don when we are heading back, cos fuck it . . .' I stated to our huddle.

'. . . Hi, excuse me, Don, sorry to bother you, we really are having a lovely time, but I'm just wondering what time we're heading back to the island?'

'Oh, Luc said everyone was staying over this evening.'

Panic struck. 'Sorry, what? No, absolutely not. We haven't brought anything with us. We thought we were just going fishing for tuna and then heading home this afternoon,' I bit back.

'Ahhh, y'see, we may have cut it too fine to get home in time, as y'see it's gonna be hard as I have to sail us through a pretty narrow crossing between the sandbar and the coral – don't wanna touch either, ya see, and it's harder to see if it's dark. That makes for some dangerous sailing.'

'We have a plane to catch in the morning from Cancún back to Sweden,' one of the Swedes with the magic-mushroom tattoo on his ankle added. Now everyone was listening. Suddenly the party didn't feel as fun. No one had intended on staying the night apart from Luc, who was nowhere to be seen.

'Where's Luc?!'

Amy, the coked-up but assertive New Yorker, added, 'Let's just go now. They have a plane to catch and we all gotta get back, it's 4.30 p.m., sundown is 7.11 p.m., and we've run out of water anyway. Surely we can make it back to shore in time?'

'Ahhh, ah, I guess if y'gotta get back y'gotta get back,' the Captain slurred, clutching onto a fresh pack of beer, visibly disappointed that his soirée with the youth had been cut short.

The three of us breathed a sigh of relief and reached for a warm cola. Tired of the sun, we sat inside, at the back of the boat, on cushioned benches behind the captain's hub, nervous, upright and ready to watch his every move, ready to assist in getting back to land.

6.30 p.m.
Above us hangs a barometer, measuring the depth of the water.

'Make sure you tell me if it goes into single digits,' Don commands with a belch. We are silent, focused and worried that if we speak, it will distract him. We are no longer in the mood to make friends. The sky moves from blue to a warm and beautiful orange glow, the sun an unwanted guest that falls towards the horizon. The wind is up as we wrap our sarongs over our shoulders and we huddle our salty skin nearer to each other. In the distance the town is twinkling as the evening sets in. We all feel sick now, desperate to make it back, checking the barometer every minute, when all of a sudden it jumps from 14 . . . 12 . . . 8 . . . 7.5 metres.

'Don, the water's low,' we sound together. He's ignoring us, sipping his warm beer, looking stressed. We carry on like this for another twenty minutes, desperate to get back on land. The 7.5-metre reading goes to 5 metres and it suddenly feels like we are slowing down, trawling through thick mud. Then there is a scraping sound below us – like a buggy trying to get over gravel – and finally an almighty thrust of the boat and a cry of 'FUCK!' from our captain.

'SON OF A BITCH!' Donald shouts to no one.

He turns off the engine, but the yacht carries on dragging through the water with the distinct sound of expensive damage.

'Has he hit the coral?' Clara mouths.

'SONOVA BITCH! GAD DAMMIT!'

Yes, we all agree.

We are now fully lodged in sand or coral, who knows? But there's a leak somewhere, as there's water trickling into the belly of the boat, right by the rudder, which is firmly stuck. We are not moving now. Our chances of getting back to land float away with the setting sun. Everyone on the boat is now paying attention, apart from Luc. There is panic. Hysteria has set in. Some people combat this by trying to help, some just take another line of cocaine. After an hour of our drunk captain trying to instruct the willing sailors of the ships on how to mend the rudder, we hear a call from the coast guards over the radio:

'Hola. Hola. Cómo estás? Necesitas ayuda?' a voice crackles through the white noise.

Donald does not reply.

'Hola. Hola. Necesitas ayuda?' Again.

'They are asking if we need help. Can you just respond to them???' Clara pleads with her A-level translation.

Donald ignores us and takes a swig of the vodka perched by his steering wheel.

The next twelve hours turn into a scene from A Perfect Storm mixed with The Comedy of Errors. A perfect induction to disaster at sea, unrolling hour by hour.

Hour 1: Gale-force winds rock the boat from side to side.

Hour 2: Screams as we are flung from one side of the boat to the other.

Hour 3: Fear.

Hour 4: Cackles and howling at the moon from the witch who has moved on to Luc's ket stash.

Hour 5: Instructions.

Hour 6: Failed instructions.

Hour 7: Water streams into the boat.

Hour 8: Luc appears blissfully numb to the panic.

Hour 9: Discussions over our impending death.

Hour 10: Drunk sea captain begins to talk to himself in the third person.

Hour 11: Clara fends off Ryan who is trying to go for a cosy comedown fondle at 3 a.m.

Hour 12: Discussions over how the *Daily Mail* will report our eventual tragic death. Alice and I decide that we will forever be immortalised as the greatest loves Jack and Sam will ever know.

6.30 a.m.
The sun begins to rise. The fisherman boats are getting ready for a day of work and in a flash the two Swedes have jumped onto one in a last-ditch attempt to get their flight.

'Take us, too!!!! Come back!' we cry on deck, exhausted, ignoring the other seven people still on board. Donald is snoring. We look down at the ocean that toyed with us so cruelly the night before. Then we realise we were never going to die. The water is the height of a toddler's paddling pool. We could have walked back to land, the water is so shallow. In the distance we see an ominous-looking boat moving towards us.

'POLICE. SHIT!' Ryan shouts to the group. 'Get rid of the drugs.'

And now we are going to be arrested and put in a Mexican jail. We wave manically at a passing small motorboat, which slows down. 'Please. Take us to land, please!' Alice yelps. Before they can even accept, Alice, Clara, the Slovakians and I have hot-stepped it onto the boat and are speeding away – away from Ryan, Amy, Luc (who is now awake), the witch and Don, who are all pouring baggies over the side of the boat before the police make it to them.

There is no remorse, no guilt about jumping off that sinking boat and saving ourselves.

We arrive on land and sway for the rest of the day, the after-shocks of being on a rocking boat for far too long.

We get to the hostel, wash, pack our bags and head for the bus station to make a swift exit out of Isla Mujeres. We will never return. But before we get on the bus, we stop at our favourite bagel shop and order the best sandwich of our lives: a large brown roll with fresh ripe avocado, perfect tomatoes, red onion and, of course, tuna.

* * *

Gaga had a group of bridge friends called 'Esther Rosen's House Party', made up of Jewish pensioners from in and around Manchester, who were looking for a good time and lots of bridge. They would travel to Fuerteventura, Bournemouth and the Algarve, pulling up to their hotel in a coach full of homemade snacks, blood-thinning tablets and Superdrug perfume.

Sometimes Mum, Hannah, Alex and I would go and visit her during school half-term, which would have my grandma beaming with pride, parading us around to different tables of chitchat.

'So *you're* Jessica! Oh, Pat's been talking about what a good singer you are and what a lovely granddaughter you are!'

'And this is Alex, who's studying for his bar mitzvah . . .' Gaga would direct the gang's gaze.

'OOOOOH, *mazel tov!*' they would say, clapping their hands. 'And where's the supermodel Hannah! We have all seen the covers of her on *Shout* and *Mizz* – what a stunner! What beautiful grandchildren you have, Pat!' Esther would project. My grandma, never shy of celebrating the small successes of her family, used to frame my sister's magazine covers and model cards for all her friends to see as soon as they walked through her flat. So if you hadn't heard about the *Just Seventeen* magazine cover, or my solo in the school musical, she would have the memorabilia to remind you.

Gaga would always tell us to get in to breakfast early so none of the others would see us taking bacon from the buffet. She didn't mind us eating it, she just didn't want the rest of the ladies 'to talk'. The hotels were always the same: a little tired, far too overheated (due to all the warfarin the guests were taking), with that fusty corridor smell of the lunch before, like mash and over-boiled veg.

We would always come to visit her near the end of the week, when she was ready to be without the hordes of elderly ailments and idle gossip. I wonder if she always felt a slight outsider, seeing as she was a convert. I never asked. Despite the European adventures, the best trips were always to Blackpool. I loved the illuminations, sitting in the car in the freezing – and wet – cold, driving through the lights, eating your fish and chips and peeking out the back window. I also loved the journey up there, as I would sneak as many tiny UHT milk cartons as possible from the train canteen to take shots back in my seat. I'd be delighted that there would be more in the hotel room next to the teas and instant coffee, along with a small pack of shortbread. If you've never actually drunk UHT milk, give it a go. Knock it back in one.

One night, on a Blackpool trip of particular adventure, we decided to get out of the hotel and go for a three-course meal and cabaret show in a place called Funny Girls. Nothing like a bit of entertainment while you eat your seasonal veg soup and bread roll and then a touch of glamour as you dig into your lamb shank on mashed potato with a wine 'jus' while a Cher number erupts onstage. Especially when it is a drag night and you're taking your eighty-five-year-old grandmother to it. This delighted the queens onstage, who shone a stage light on her as she had her bread and butter pudding in the booth and squealed over the microphone, 'We've got a Funny Girls virgin in the house!!!' To which my grandma offered her most regal wave back to the hollering applause from the room.

The Bar Mitzvah

It was what my mum had been working towards ever since he arrived in 1987; finally, Lennie had a son of age! A beautiful boy to bar mitzvah!

At this point we had only ever been to a couple of bar mitzvah's, both of which had been Jill Reichman's boys: Gary's back in 1996, and Jeremy's in 1999. I found it fascinating being at Norrice Lea Orthodox Synagogue up in Hampstead Garden Suburb, where the women sat at the top and the men in the main atrium. It was different to our temple, Wimbledon Shul – far grander and huge. For Gary's evening 'do', his parents, Jill and Phillip, had contemplated paying Ryan Giggs a sizeable fee to come to the reception for ten minutes, shake Gary's hand and say 'mazel tov', but they opted for The Bootleg Beatles. We had lunch in a marquee at their house in the suburbs, then we changed into new evening outfits in anticipation of a late night at the Four Seasons hotel on Park Lane. It was the most fabulous night of my life. Jill always knew how to do things fabulously, like when she organised a limousine for us to go and see Kylie

Minogue at the Docklands back in 1991. I was six and had a new H&M ensemble on: nineties splatted fluorescent florals on blue trousers and a matching blouse.

At Gary's bar mitzvah, for the first time I was surrounded by a room *full* of Jewish people, and I felt elated. I was among a tribe that I instinctively felt part of. Even though I knew very little about the guests, there was an unsaid understanding and closeness to each and every person in that room. I started my podcast, *Table Manners*, out of a love for my Jewish heritage and to celebrate our unorthodox yet ritualistic Friday-night Dinners. Our family's approach to Shabbat would see candles lit, Hebrew blessings rushed and a lot of chicken variations, before finishing the night dancing to Whitney around the table with our non-Jewish friends. Being a South-London Jew was seen as something 'exotic' in my younger years. My grandma gave me a Star of David, and I'd proudly wear it around my neck; a beautiful sign of my heritage, but also a reminder that I wasn't quite the same as all my friends. I loved going up to Hampstead Garden Suburbs to the Reichmans', for Rosh Hashanah or Passover, where everyone would shout over each other in a chaotic but comforting and familiar way. However, when it came to understanding my heritage, the religion and Jewish history, I was far too sociable and too busy to practise for a bat mitzvah at thirteen. Weekend shul became an inconvenience to my budding social life and I avoided going.

* * *

While my dyslexic little brother Alex worked day and night decoding Hebrew, Mum, Hannah and I planned the party. My brother was a willing and obedient son, a 'good Jewish boy' with a limited social life to interfere with chada (Hebrew school) on a Sunday morning. The priorities were: food, entertainment, outfits, change of outfits, guest list, venues, tans and finally but lowest on the list was Alex actually reading a portion of the Torah. Mum rented a sunbed for two weeks prior to the event and we set it up in Alex's old room, replenishing our glow through the dark days of the November drear and gloom.

It was the new millennium, and Mum was determined to go against the grain with the theme of the party. Bar mitzvahs are *always* themed. David Schwimmer told us on the podcast that his was magic themed, which must be a thing for American Jews as so was Benny Blanco's. Jordan Firstman's was *Wicked! The Musical*. But for little Alex, we were all to travel to the world of North Africa. We were having a Moroccan-themed bar mitzvah.

We had, I should say, zero ties to Morocco. We weren't even Sephardi Jews, who originate from that part of the world. Alex had only started eating food other than spaghetti bolognese and cucumber sandwiches a few years prior. But Mum and Alex went off to the caterers to test the tagines, scoff all the canapés and cake, then peg it to Calais to buy the wine. Mum even hired a venue stylist – our own version of Frank from *Father of the Bride*.

'Bouquets are *so* passé!' Frank said. So, for our centrepiece on the tables, we had decapitated flower heads floating in water-filled blue-glass fish bowls. Together, Mum and the sadistic stylist decided we should have a little dinner entertainment, too. Mum dialled up the Internet and typed keywords into the Yahoo search engine! Our guests' meals were to be accompanied by a mysterious woman by the name of Zanouba, who would shimmy along the lines of tables in between the tagine and pud to add a little exotica to the evening. What actually turned up on the night was a very pale middle-aged lady called Dawn from Essex, who had a huge appendix scar on her perfectly wobbly tummy and danced with a machete in her mouth. Not the taste of *Arabian Nights* we had been expecting, but perhaps the one we deserved.

After the dinner we had the discotheque, and the mother-and-son first dance. I kid you not. We had gone back and forth over the song, I wanted 'I Love Your Smile' by Shanice, Mum wanted 'Mad About the Boy' (of course she did), but in the end we settled on Toploader's 'Dancing in the Moonlight'. Watching them dance was perfect joy – little Alex all suited and booted in his oversized Next suit, looking up at our adoring mother. I was feeling fabulous with my tan, my Topshop red satin bodice (inspired by Posh Spice) and Miss Selfridge black bootlegs. I was also knocking back drinks poured by my friend George Roberts, who'd accepted bar duty for twenty quid, coaxed along by his mother, who was the caterer. Inevitably, those drinks had a 3:1 ratio of alcohol to soft drink. We were reeling from the booze and S Club 7's 'Reach for the Stars', a ubiquitous bar mitzvah song during the early noughties. Glittery wigs and plastic sunglasses were thrown out by the DJ to all the revellers before we thrust my completely inebriated little brother up in the sky on a chair. The image was this: tinsel wig skew-whiff, a sweaty beetroot face from the sunbed, holding onto a Magnum Mini with a slight look of fear behind his glazed eyes.

* * *

Next year I will have my own bat mitzvah, aged thirty-seven, and only now am I beginning to understand and appreciate the weight of it. The thought of a Jewish ceremony was a visceral reaction to rising anti-Semitism. Somewhere down the line, I had stopped wearing my Star of David, toned down the 'Jew' in me, brushed Jew-hate under the carpet, even when it was directed at me. I had forgotten that when I started out in music, there were swastikas lining the comments under my YouTube videos and discussions about the size of my nose. My mother was horrified and reported them, while I told her to 'just leave it'. There are probably more but I've stopped looking. And now, in 2020, a year that will never be forgotten, I ask myself: why did it feel hard to look the Jew-hate in the eye?

Suddenly I began to feel scared about my heritage and culture being rejected, abandoned and potentially eradicated. So where do I now fit in? In the same place – I now understand – as many other Jews: I don't want my heritage to become so politicised, but I want to challenge the anti-Semitism that is rooted in 3,000 years of Jewish history. Jews have endured and survived, but they'll only do so by acknowledging the modern manifestations of Jew-hate, however loudly or quietly they lurk. Anti-Semitism attempts to rot a generation – my generation – with vicious fallacy. And I won't have it.

I still don't know if I believe in a God – I'm not sure any of my family do – and I don't seek to express my Judaism in simple faith. Instead, I want to celebrate my identity, confidently express my tribe and understand it better, and for me to pass all of that on to my children. It has always been there, in my blood, but it has always been somewhat out of reach as well. So I decided to walk the walk and study for a bat mitzvah. It will be very different to Alex's, and I hope with my age comes a different offering to the experience. I'll enjoy choosing the portion of the Torah I will read and highlighting the significance of it, with my thirty-six years of lived experience. I have the same teacher as my brother had, Aviva (who was babysat by Gaga in Manchester), a friend and inspiring poet and academic, who encourages me to question the Torah, to debate it with respect. Yes, my kids will love the party. Perhaps my friends and family will be slightly confused and think I'm 'born again'. Will I have a first dance with my mum? Yes, and I might even get my very own Frank to plan it.

In the future, maybe *I* will be the proud mother kvelling at my children's bat mitzvah or bar mitzvah, or maybe they just won't fancy it. But they will have an understanding of our culture and my Jewish faith, and they will be able to make that choice for themselves. A bar mitzvah or bat mitzvah is a Jewish coming-of-age ceremony. Finally, at thirty-six, I'm ready to fully embrace and respect this world that has given me so much intangible pride, purpose and love. And the spread *will* be excellent.

Milk

I remember being sad about something; it was the evening and I was watching telly in the playroom. I was about nine, it was nearly bedtime and my mum could see I was upset. She introduced me to the greatest – perhaps excessive – pleasure in life: cream on ice cream. As I spooned the white-on-white sugar into my mouth, everything else slipped away. That bedtime bowl of cream nullified the sadness. In fact, I have forgotten whatever I was sad about in the first place; now that memory is purely about the discovery of such a great pairing.

When I got my period, aged eleven, in our chalet in Abersoch, Wales – the summer holiday before starting secondary school – it was a Wispa Gold that accompanied the sanitary pads on Mum's return from the tearful drive to the shops.

When I was poorly and lost my voice before having to sing in the school musical, aged sixteen, it was chicken soup and hot Vimto that remedied this.

I was thirteen when Dad told us he was having another child with a different woman, Clare rushed over with Jack and we ordered an Indian takeaway. The mums drank wine and we danced the hurt away. Food resolved tears, heartache, stress and sadness and, least importantly, hunger. Eating was celebrated in our house; it was an extension of my mother's love, the essence of our family life. Food was made to be respected and it was offered up as a solution to any problem.

CREAM ON ICE CREAM

Double cream
Häagen-Dazs Pralines & Cream ice cream

1. *Pour the double cream over the scoops of ice cream generously. If you're not quick in eating it and lucky enough, you may get newly formed cold clumps of double cream that dot the ice cream, which are heavenly.*

* * *

I learnt to eat and enjoy food through my mum, and waited for that moment when I would become a mum and could pass down all her wisdom. And that would start when I breastfed my baby for the first time. Apart from the bleeding nipples, Mum had said it was an absolute cinch. She was incredibly proud of how long she had breastfed us all. With my first pregnancy, I was blindly confident, barely thinking about feeding my unborn child. I had done so much preparation for the birth, I hadn't really thought about the 'looking after the baby' part. I presumed I would be a total natural, as it had always been my main ambition to become a mother, my mum had found it easy and the apple didn't fall far from the tree. My daughter was born and she was on my boob within minutes. So far so good. When we returned home the next day, she was plugged into me day and night, constantly feeding, constantly sleeping. And initially I loved it, even through the wincing of cracked nipples. But as the first week went by, she was never off my chest; her tiny features contorted like a tormented creature that banged her head at me, frustrated and angry at my broken nipple when she couldn't find it quick enough to feed.

'Oh, the witching hour, it's a thing!' I read on Mumsnet. From 3 p.m. until 12 a.m. I would be sat on the sofa with my exasperated, hungry newborn and a sustenance station: a stool with a litre bottle of water, lukewarm tea, fenugreek tablets and a microwave meal. While my milk lacked in abundance, my armpits would seep out the overpowering smell of fenugreek, a sinking reminder of what felt like failure.

'This is so strange, I used to just be able to feed on one boob for ten minutes for all of you,' Mum would say over the phone if she was checking in, or holler from the kitchen while she made me bowls of hot food.

'Well, obviously that's not the case for me, Mum. Thanks a lot,' I snapped back.

'It shouldn't be this hard, darling.'

'They say it takes six weeks to get going with breastfeeding. I'm on week four and it's getting harder, Mum. She's so hungry and I can't express more than 20ml. I'm so tired, I stink of curry and I can't drink anymore Guinness. And then I see all my mates with their leaking boobs and all talking about the tingle you're meant to get for the 'let-down'. I get nothing! Breastfeeding is the fucking let-down.' I ranted and raved and ignored the obvious solution.

* * *

'Breast is best' is repeated to you as soon as you get pregnant. 'Do you breastfeed?' is what the health visitor asks you straight away, as you sit down with your new bundle. At one breastfeeding clinic, a breastfeeding advisor had told me to set my alarm every two hours during the night to feed my daughter to get my milk to flow better. But on the off chance that she was going to sleep for over two hours, I certainly wasn't going to wake myself up when my daughter was already doing a great job of that herself. I was overwhelmed by the cruelly evangelical prescriptions made by so many women around me. So, what was the other option if your baby was losing weight and you were trying your best but your best didn't seem to be working? I meekly asked a midwife at a weigh-in if I should consider topping up her feeds with a bottle of formula. 'Breast is best, but if you really want to, go ahead.'

That night my hungry baby had her first bottle of formula in the evening and finally I saw what people had talked about. She was 'milk drunk', satisfied and full. I cried as Sam and I watched her down the whole bottle in one without a pause; a small admission of defeat but evidence that I was doing the right thing and taking my first decisive steps as her mother.

This did not stop me getting paranoid and embarrassed when I took a bottle out in public. I felt the judgment of the coffee-shop worker, the milk-laden mothers in a baby singing class, or even my dry cleaner who would baldly say, 'I hope you're breast-feeding,' when I came to pick up my laundry. 'Er, yes, I am mix-feeding, as I was really struggling with breastfeeding . . . I didn't produce enough mi—' I trailed off. Why was I explaining myself to a lady I didn't know, who had already shrunk a really nice mohair jumper of mine?

I had accepted that my boobs were not made for fully feeding a child and I would remind myself that offering my daughter breast milk before filling her up on formula was simply the same as enjoying a pre-dinner amuse-bouche, a starter or a side salad. And while I was quite jealous of the women who had dark circles staining their T-shirts, a 'fast flow' or who expressed enough milk to feed a village, I accepted that finally my child was thriving. You would have thought this would stop me obsessing over it all again with child number two. Instead, I went down a deeper rabbit hole, determined to right the wrongs of my first experience. I started believing that I hadn't been able to feed my daughter due to working too hard, not bonding well enough, putting too much stress on myself and pushing a bottle on her too quickly. My new baby came with a second chance to master the feeding.

* * *

The main image I have of those first two weeks with my newborn son is of a woman in bed, all day, convinced it was necessary for breastfeeding, in what I presume were the initial stages of postnatal depression.

I sat there in bed with my perfect little boy, eating mounds of homemade breastfeeding oat cookies, washing them down with a morning, mid-afternoon or evening breastfeeding Lotus biscoff-flavoured milkshake, banging back a couple of fenugreek tablets every so often after a bowl of soup (I heard soup was good for the flow). I was Regina George from *Mean Girls*, locked into a protein-bar habit of my own making. I was optimistic at the start, thinking of it as a challenge to complete, a mountain to conquer.

I had an app to time the feeds: right breast fifty minutes, left breast fifty-seven minutes.

I had the lactation consultant come and show me how to feed him with an extra-tiny feeding tube of expressed milk while he still sucked on my breast, so as not to diminish my breast milk production.

I had the hospital-grade pump that was so strong it would make my nipples the size and length of a Celebrations Twix.

I had the homeopathic remedies, and the prescribed medicine, too. Pill upon pill, advice upon more advice. If I wasn't feeding him, I was pumping, and if I wasn't pumping, I was talking to Sam about feeding our son or whether he was tongue-tied or not or whether he seemed satisfied. I was obsessed, manic and couldn't leave the house, unless it was to go to a breastfeeding clinic. Everyone supported me and my fixation on trying to get it working differently this time. But quietly I think they were worried, and my incredibly supportive midwives would not discharge me until they saw more weight gain on him. Or maybe it was because they thought I was low, I'm not sure.

Nothing was helping. I didn't wash much, I didn't pay my daughter any attention and I punished myself for not cracking it this time round. I felt numb and floated around in a silent grey fog. My fixation on nourishing my child had moved beyond reasonable care into a maddening, anxious repetition. While I had the determination to keep going, it was becoming detrimental to my mental health and everyone I loved around me.

It was Mum and Sam who intervened and begged me to feed him some formula. And I immediately felt released. Relieved. I just needed someone else to make that decision for me.

* * *

Some people have straightforward births – I did – and some don't. Some people will find breastfeeding the most wonderful thing, others will find it unnatural, brutal and impossible. Even though I have now made peace with it, I'm still somewhat haunted by the time I lost with my newborn babies, wasting precious moments when I could have been marvelling at these perfect masterpieces, all because I was too busy torturing myself that the same body that grew them was not enough to help them thrive. Formula was a gift to my babies and me. It was the vital hand that helped us. I am now waiting for my third and I will feel no fear or guilt for that first day we meet. I'll have my boobs ready, and a box of formula and a sterilised bottle waiting close by.

Eggs

I remember when we were little, my mum would set out 'midnight feasts' for us, which weren't eaten at midnight at all, but at 6 a.m. on a Saturday morning. She would put out our red plastic table and chairs in the living room, with individually cling-filmed paper plates of Iced Gems, slices of apple, a peeled satsuma and raisins. We would creep downstairs with whoever had slept over, filling our tummies with sugar watching *The Racoons* or *Fraggle Rock* on the television. Our friends would revel in the breakfast mezze and hours of telly, only to enjoy a fry-up a few hours later of beef or chicken sausages (it was Shabbat, after all), fried eggs, beans and tinned plum tomatoes that made the brown toast soggy. We didn't realise at the time that these feasts were just to ensure that Mum got a few more uninterrupted hours in bed. I worked that one out thirty years later, when I was a mother myself.

* * *

During my mum's childhood, olive oil was only available at the chemist. I take for granted how much I depend on olive oil and how malleable it is, whether as a dip for fresh bread, generously drizzled on anything going into the oven, added to a cake or used as baking paper (because who has the time to faff around cutting parchment into the shape of a cake tin?). While there is plenty that is medicinal about the miraculous nectar, I don't advise using olive oil as a tan enhancer or sun protector, especially as you climb the Acropolis on the last day of your holiday. You may want to beat Alice in the back-to-school tan wars, but you will discover on descent that blisters will have appeared on your aspirins-on-an-ironing-board chest (looking more the colour of ibuprofen now), peaking over your lilac dyed cotton vest with a hot pink lace trim that you bought from Camden Lock on the first day of the summer holidays. You should, however, use olive oil to fry the crispiest egg of your life.

A FRIED EGG

Plenty of olive oil

1 egg

1. *Get the olive oil hotter than the Athens August sun and crack the egg into the frying pan. Watch in delight as the whites bubble and turn brown and crispy.*

* * *

Nine-year-old Zoe was in love with Luke Perry. So, if Zoe was in love, then I, her best friend, followed suit. She was the matriarch of our quartet at primary school: the oldest, the wisest, the brightest star. Her parents had split up and she had a schedule that split her time between her mum's and dad's homes. Thursday after school was handover time, until Saturday at around 4 p.m. My parents hadn't separated when we met, so to me it was an alluring prospect, having two bedrooms, two bedtimes, two different fridges. Both had infinite competitive treats, from watching a film slightly too old for us at her dad's, or ice cream sundaes by her mum followed by perfectly buttery scrambled eggs with tomato ketchup in the morning. I was a spoilt guest.

Our sleepovers were spent watching the *Buffy the Vampire Slayer* film on repeat. On a Friday night, we would go down to our local shop and video rental place on Abbeville Road, Treohans, renewing another week to overdose on Luke, banana Nesquik in tall glasses or peach iced tea Snapple. We searched for anything to do with Luke Perry, all American or Americana, our prepubescent hormones sounding a tiny alarm in the form of an infatuation with baseball jackets, dream boys and diners. If Zoe got a baseball jacket with leather sleeves for her tenth birthday in September, by 15 October I knew what I would be expecting, only in a different colour. The one crush we disagreed on was which Take That member to adorn our bedroom walls with. She went for Mark; I was devoted to Robbie. Zoe was the leader and I was her willing student.

My sister wanted Ed's Easy Diner for her 12th birthday, but I asked for Rock Island Café for my 10th birthday celebration in London's Trocadero. Zoe had hosted her birthday dinner there the month before, why else?

Rock Island Café was much like Ed's Easy Diner. Hidden away on the second floor of the Trocedero, it had shiny Formica countertops and blockbuster burgers, juke boxes filled with 1950s music and a desirable malted milkshake. It also had 'The Dinettes', the waiters and waitresses dressed in white rolled-up T-shirts, paper hats and pulled-up socks who wore roller skates. Midway through your meal, they would jump up onto the counters and perform the *Grease* medley or something equally

exhilarating to a ten-year-old Zoe and Jessie. It looked so much fun – all I wanted to do was work as a waitress with my hair in a bouncy pony tail, listening to Buddy Holly or the Fontane Sisters, with my pen and pad, shuffling around saying, 'What can I get ya?' There is barely anything about Rock Island Café on the Internet, with Planet Hollywood eclipsing its status, but I did find a YouTube video of The Dinettes dancing. I don't remember them being so nonchalant and underwhelming at the time.

Still riding high on the USA, movies and Nickelodeon, we would return to the Trocadero time and time again in those days, an utterly selfless act of love on my mum's part. The Trocadero was a horrendous place, but to a little person it was overwhelmingly futuristic and tantalising, offering an unhealthy taste of capitalism with its flashing lights, high prices, commercialism and gargantuan pitch in the centre of London. Mum was about to split up with my father – something we had no idea about; maybe she didn't either. She would take six or more children out with an ease only slightly tempered by exhaustive shouting – but it never seemed too hard to her. We were spoilt. Spoilt by her joie de vivre, even when she had nothing to be joyful about at the Trocadero. And spoilt by the supersized gobstoppers or dummy sweets she'd buy us before we entered Alien War. It was something close to an escape room, where you 'fought' your way out of a spaceship in the middle of an 'alien attack'. I will never forget seeing grown men push little children out of the way to escape.

Mum took us to Planet Hollywood, also at the Trocadero, for my eleventh birthday dinner, where I got a huge birthday cake with the Planet Hollywood sign emblazoned on the top. Around the table – among Arnie and Bruce memorabilia – sat Mum, Hannah, Alex and Zoe. It was noisy and exhausting, and I felt a little sorry for Mum having to return to this place again and again. Although it was *the* place to go as an eleven-year-old, it never hit the spot like the charming Rock Island Café had done. Even in a room filled with caricatured Hollywood, prizes and prices ostentatiously dripping off the walls, I would have preferred the malted milkshake for half the price at the tucked-away diner on the floor below. Maybe it was me growing up, growing out of my love affair with the movies; maybe it was me developing a small level of taste. I'm not too sure.

* * *

You can't make an omelette without breaking a few eggs.

'Are you hungry, darling, shall I make you an omelette?'

'Stop offering me omelettes, I don't want an omelette, Mum!'

Everything always comes back to the omelette, much to my brother's despair. I actually quite like having an omelette made by my mother. It's always slightly overdone but always considered, generous in cheese and well seasoned.

She will offer you an omelette at any given time. First thing in the morning, late at night if you have arrived at the house and she hasn't made dinner. If there is a crisis, there is the offer of an omelette.

My grandfather, Mor Mor, used to make a mean omelette with Bloom's Salami. Mor Mor called it 'vorscht' but actually I think that was just his Yiddish pronunciation of the German word for sausage 'wurst' that stuck with the family. Bloom's salami is a kosher salami, wide in girth and puce coloured, yet strangely it is still a beef sausage. Kind of like a saveloy. Anything with eggs was his forte: matzo Brie, challah eggy bread, any kind of omelette. He couldn't cook, but he was always in charge of the eggs.

'I don't know if you have ever actually made me one,' Alex said.

'Because you never bloody want one!' she said.

It was 1994 and a typical Sunday, bleak and grey, the time when a crisis always seems to fall. Dad was moving out of the family house. He wasn't sure if it was permanent or not.

Before he left, he asked my mum if he could make an omelette. She kindly let him. She drew the line at him taking the whisk away with him.

She still offers up an omelette at any opportunity. And even if my brother won't take up the offer, I always will.

Acknowledgements

Thank you to all my friends and family for our memories and meals together.

To my husband for giving me my favourite love story, ever.

To my children for constantly levelling me and my gastronomical fervour. Here's to eating a tomato in the near future. I love you.

To Harriet Poland for being the most outstanding publisher and editor and holding my hand every step of the way, and to everyone at Hodder Studio.

To Charlie Brotherstone, for convincing me to write this book (dare I say it, a Foodoir!)

To Izzy Everington, thanks for making editing the book such a pain free endeavour.

To Coco Bayley, for the most fabulous cover!

To Peter Loraine, Sarah Jackson, Adam Klein and Kirsty Richardson for being my wonderful cheerleaders and such constant support.

Finally, to my insatiable appetite, thank you for everything.